SpringerBriefs in Psychology

SpringerBriefs in Theoretical Advances in Psychology

SpringerBriefs present concise summaries of cutting-edge research and practical applications across a wide spectrum of fields. Featuring compact volumes of 55 to 125 pages, the series covers a range of content from professional to academic. Typical topics might include:

- A timely report of state-of-the-art analytical techniques
- A bridge between new research results as published in journal articles and a contextual literature review
- A snapshot of a hot or emerging topic
- An in-depth case study or clinical example
- A presentation of core concepts that readers must understand to make independent contributions

SpringerBriefs in Psychology showcase emerging theory, empirical research, and practical application in a wide variety of topics in psychology and related fields. Briefs are characterized by fast, global electronic dissemination, standard publishing contracts, standardized manuscript preparation and formatting guidelines, and expedited production schedules.

Series Editors

Jaan Valsiner, Aalborg University, Aalborg, Denmark

Carlos Cornejo, Escuela de Psicologia, Pontificia Universidad Católica de Chile Santiago, Macul, Chile

SpringerBriefs in Theoretical Advances in Psychology will be an extension from the currently renovated Annals of Theoretical Psychology in the direction of bringing short, single (or multiple) authored theoretical advancements across all areas of psychology to the international audience. The focus is on the development of innovative theoretical approaches and their discussion. The Series will have a clearly defined international and interdisciplinary focus – even if it remains within the discipline of psychology.

Featuring compact volumes of 100 to 115 pages, each Brief in the Series is meant to provide a clear, visible, and multi-sided recognition of the theoretical efforts of scholars around the world. It is targeted to researchers, graduate students, and professionals in Post-BA level psychology, education, anthropology, and sociology.

Briefs are published as part of the Springer's eBook collection, with millions of users worldwide. In addition, Briefs are available for individual print and electronic purchase.

Fathali M. Moghaddam

The Psychology
of Multiculturalism,
Assimilation,
and Omniculturalism

Managing Diversity in Global Context

 Springer

Fathali M. Moghaddam (iD)
Department of Psychology
White Gravenor Hall
Georgetown University
Washington, DC, USA

ISSN 2192-8363   ISSN 2192-8371   (electronic)
SpringerBriefs in Psychology
ISSN 2511-395X   ISSN 2511-3968   (electronic)
SpringerBriefs in Theoretical Advances in Psychology
ISBN 978-3-031-62596-1   ISBN 978-3-031-62597-8   (eBook)
https://doi.org/10.1007/978-3-031-62597-8

This Springer imprint is published by the registered company Springer Nature Switzerland AG
The registered company address is: Gewerbestrasse 11, 6330 Cham, Switzerland

If disposing of this product, please recycle the paper.

This book is dedicated to my mother and father, and to the next generation, Nikoo and Guilan.

Series Editors' Preface

Unity in Diversity: Omniculturalism as the Axiomatic Basis for Psychology

Fathali Moghaddam accomplishes a long-awaited axiomatic change in scientific psychology in this little book. He points out that the necessary focus for psychology is not the study of inter-individual differences but exactly their opposite—inter-individual similarities. He proves eloquently how the appealing focus on multiculturalism in psychology—based on the focus on differences between majority and minority groups, or of different societies—are the basis for societal outcomes that psychologists sincerely desire to eliminate. When one finds a difference between two groups (A and B), the particular meaning of the difference is turned from scientific neutrality to ideologically laden evaluation—A is seen not just as *different* from B but *better than* B. This subtle value insertion leads easily to stigmatization of the other group, polarization that leads to conflict, and—eventually—to genocides. This unfortunate potential inherent in psychologists' habitual discoveries of differences is deeply disconcerting, even as a remote possibility. Moghaddam contrasts multiculturalism with omniculturalism. While the former seeks to build an initially non-existent unity from the differences observed, the latter, on the contrary, actively and primarily conceives the unity, to refer to the differences only later (and only if pertinent). Thus, while multiculturalism assumes the challenge of constructing a community that tacitly is presumed to be non-existent, omniculturalism, through a perceptual Gestalt turn, makes the community pre-exist to the group differences that matter to social scientists.

Bad habits are hard to break—especially when these are supported by social norms. The proliferation of statistical methods turned into theory (Gigerenzer, 1991) has turned the discovery of differences into the expected outcome of empirical research. The changing methodological fashions in the twentieth-century psychology—moving away from single-case based phenomenology to large sample research (Toomela and Valsiner, 2010). The normative use of statistical methods to ascertain differences works precisely against the first step of omniculturalism—the focus on similarity behind the established difference. The statistical paradigm is incapable to focus on similarities. New perspectives—especially qualitative rigorous methodologies (Rudolph, 2013)—need to replace the reliance on statistical generalization. Psychological phenomena are qualitative in their nature, and their quantification is an operation that eliminates the very phenomena by replacing them by what is believed to be their "measures" (Michell, 1999). What we habitually refer to as "measurement" of psychological characteristics entails projection of causal powers into the person without any substantiation. An accumulation of a person's answers on a "introversion scale" is projected into the person—whose shyness in social context is then interpreted as if caused by *introversion* as a supposedly causal entity.

Moghaddam in this book sets up the sequence for omnicultural understanding— first figure out in what ways you are similar to the Other, and *only after that* focus on the features that are different between you and the Other. The focus on similarity helps to understand the universal way of being human—despite all differences, human beings are similar to one another. He does not specify how precisely this unification of the universal core of similarity and the individual specific features takes place. For understanding that process, we need to go back two centuries—and look carefully at the very birth of the dialectical triad of THESIS → ANTITHESIS → SYNTHESIS that was created by Johann Gottlieb Fichte at the time of his entering into professorship at the University of Jena (Fichte, 1794, pp. 35–37). Fichte's crucial role in the development of that triad—and its component of double negation—has been left in the shadow of the dialectical mystifications by Georg Friedrich Wilhelm Hegel during the decades after Fichte had been expelled from academic world of Jena.

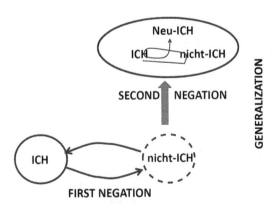

Fig. 1 Fichte's notion of two negations and generalization

Fichte—a talented preacher whose ideas captured student audiences in his few years (1794–1799) in Jena—started from positing the duality of the Self (Ich in contrast with Nicht-Ich) that made it possible to look at similarities and differences. Differently from Moghaddam two centuries later, Fichte started from first discovering the difference (Ich <different from> nicht-Ich). This difference specified the first negation (Ich is not non-Ich). Our psychology that has habitually discovered differences stops at this stage.

Fichte, however, proceeded beyond the first negation. In his concept of second negation, the first negation is negated (e.g., while it is true that Ich <is different> from non-Ich, that difference does not matter). The second negation leads to generalization beyond the first negation, re-uniting the different parts of the Self in the bounded structure that is a new synthesis of the parts (Fig. 1).

Fichte did not develop his theoretical system of double negation further after his exit from academia, and neither have other dialectically minded philosophers after him elaborated that concept. Interestingly, in the present book, Moghaddam uses the process of synthesis in the direction opposite to Fichte's—first discover the similarity (which matters) then add to it the differences. This stems from the general humanistic focus of the author who deeply cares about the never-ending political and societal turmoils that explode all around the World. Unity by conquest that has proliferated in history (Chap. 8) needs to be replaced by unity of feeling into the Other (*Einfühlung*). At this point, Moghaddam's quest for similarities converges with the pluralism originally defended at the end of the eighteenth century by Johann Gottfried Herder—whose work in many ways defined the traits of the anti-rationalistic thinking of the nineteenth century (Berlin, 1999). Herder did not only accept the multiplicity of cultures, but he also defended their incommensurability, so that it is not possible to understand the values, aesthetics, and customs of an alien culture if applying a standardized cannon. In that case, we could only describe such alien culture by means of negative terms (non-Western, non-rational, non-industrialized, etc.). Every culture ought to be described from within (instead from the outside) if we really wish to understand them as human creations. Similarly, Moghaddam's invitation is to apprehend the Other from the perspective of a similar one, one who has had developed tools (some equal, some different) to surmount the same problems that every human being must face.

Here starts the positive program for human development that builds upon the differences as these feed forward into the unification of the past and future aspirations. Omnicultural contrasts are the basis for proculturation theory (Gamsakhurdia, 2022) which looks at the synthesis of the human mind moving toward the future as part of the "minority group" of migrants.

What unites the two thinkers—Fichte and Moghaddam—across the two centuries and the cultural-historical contexts of Germany and Persia is the focus on the *whole structural unity* of the person. This focus has been lost in psychology over its transformations in the twentieth century, and replaced by elementaristic and

accumulational efforts to re-construct the human mind from elements, not consider-
ing the bonds between them that make the systemic (Gestalt) quality of the whole.
Omniculturalism is the general framework that restores the primacy of the whole—
the human psyche as a system that transforms itself, in constant relating with the
environment.

Vienna, Austria   Jaan Valsiner
Santiago de Chile, Chile   Carlos Cornejo

References

Berlin, I. (1999). *The roots of romanticism*. Princeton University Press.
Fichte, J. G. (1794). *Grundlage der gesammten Wissenschaftslehre als Handschrift für eine Zuhöre*r. Christian Ernst Gabler.
Gamsakhurdia, V. L. (2022). *Theory of proculturation: Development of the self in intercultural communication*. Springer.
Gigerenzer, G. (1991). From tools to theories: A heuristic of discovery in cognitive psychology. *Psychological Review, 98*, 254–267.
Michell, J. (1999). *Measurement in psychology*. Cambridge University Press.
Rudoph, L. (ed.). (2013). *Qualitative mathematics for the social sciences*. Routledge.
Toomela, A., & Valsiner, J. (eds.). (2010). *Methodological thinking in psychology: 60 years gone astray?* Information Age Publishers.

Preface

We can predict with certainty that societies will become more diverse over the next century, and so the challenge of how to best manage diversity will become more important. In this book, I identify the serious shortcomings of multiculturalism and assimilation, the dominant approaches to diversity management, and put forward omniculturalism as a far better approach.

An ideal is the most practical thing; it moves us to try to improve the world. Omniculturalism presents an ideal that can unite all humanity to work for a better world, using as a point of departure the simple fact that humans are in foundational ways far more similar to each another than they are different. In a world where human similarities are given priority and celebrated, and differences are assigned a secondary role, we become more inclined to treat everyone as members of one group, humanity. Omniculturalism best incapsulates the interests and needs of both minority and majority groups.

Multiculturalism has served minority group elites very well, but it has failed to benefit non-elite minority group members. This reality is reflected in the plight of non-elite minority populations, especially in domains such as educational performance, political power, and material wealth. Neither has multiculturalism benefited majority group members, who in general have ended up feeling ambivalent toward multiculturalism. Assimilation has for the most part benefitted majority groups, but not minority groups. In contrast, omniculturalism will benefit all humanity and represents an ideal to guide our future actions.

Washington, DC, USA   Fathali M. Moghaddam

Acknowledgment

I am deeply indebted to my former mentors, Leslie S. Hearnshaw, David Canter, Peter Stringer, and Rom Harré. I also want to thank Jaan Valsiner, who continues to move psychology in progressive directions.

Contents

Chapter 1
Rethinking Our Future Together: Meeting the Challenge of Managing Diversity and Inclusion in the Twenty-First Century

Family is a varied and splendid thing. Among people in Kinnaur, Western Himalaya, *fraternal polyandry* is practiced, where one woman marries a man and his brothers.[1] Children have one mother and (if the husband has brothers) multiple fathers, all the fathers being brothers. According to the practices of Shi'a Islam, who mostly live in Afghanistan, Iraq, Iran, and Pakistan, a man can have four regular "permanent" wives, as well as numerous temporary ones.[2] Actually, there are no limits to the number of temporary wives a Shi'a Muslim man can have (a Shi'a Muslim woman can only have one husband, permanent or temporary). In a Shi'a Muslim marriage, children have one father, but multiple women could play the role of mothers, some of them possibly being temporary wives. In the United States and many other Western democratic societies, a married couple can consist of a man and a woman, or two women or two men, in the role of husband and wife.[3] In these cases, the role of mother and/or father would be filled by one man and one woman, or two men, or two women. Many other combinations have evolved, such as one gay woman being the husband of two gay wives—so the children have one woman serving the role of father and two women serving the role of mother.

It is easy to become mesmerized by these kinds of surface differences, and to lose sight of what really makes a family at the deepest level. Yes, there are some cross-cultural differences in the combinations of males and females serving as parents in marriages, as well as arrangements for taking care of children. Yes, there are differences in whether the man and wife are the same or different sexes, and how many of each sex there are in the marriage. But these are surface differences. At a

---

[1] Rahimzadeh (2020).

[2] Haeri (2014).

[3] I am using the terms "man" and "woman" to refer to how a person was registered at birth, noting that this labeling might be changed at a later time.

F. M. Moghaddam, *The Psychology of Multiculturalism, Assimilation, and Omniculturalism*, SpringerBriefs in Psychology, https://doi.org/10.1007/978-3-031-62597-8_1

deeper level, what really matters and *what ultimately makes a family* are core characteristics that prove to be universal and ever-present.

All families are made up of individuals who love one another, take care of one another, sacrifice for one another, show loyalty to one another, trust one another, forgive one another, and dedicate themselves to improving the lives of family members. Throughout our long evolutionary history, the family (in different shapes and formulations) remains the basic stable unit that has ensured human survival, by successfully raising the next generation and increasing the probability of our collective continuation. Marriage is one of the oldest and most widely spread human institutions.[4] The slogan that best captures the love, support, sacrifice, loyalty, trust, forgiveness, and dedication characteristic of all functioning human families around the world is "all for one, and one for all."[5]

Just as surface differences can distract us from the deep similarities that exist across all human families in societies around the world, we can be misled to focus on surface differences across ethnic groups, language groups, sexual orientation groups, religious groups, nationalities, and the many other types of groups that thrive in the global human community (note that I did not mention "racial" groups, and I shall explain this omission later in this chapter). But instead of being distracted by surface differences, we should appreciate and concentrate on the much deeper similarities shared by the members of all human groups. Yes, there are surface differences across groups in how people dress, the languages they speak, how they prepare and present food, the music they listen to, the color of their skins, the shapes of their bodies, and even some of their values, attitudes, norms, and many other such characteristics. However, at a deeper level, human beings across all groups are far more similar to one another than they are different. The core essence of what makes us human is shared by everyone in all groups across the globe.

A number of researchers have systematically examined and mapped out human universals, with Donald Brown making particularly important contributions.[6] Brown's simple list of examples of human universals is an excellent point of departure for us, "In the cultural realm, human universals include myths, legends, daily routines, rules, concepts of luck and precedent, body adornment, and the use and production of tools; in the realm of language, universals include grammar, phonemes, polysemy, metonymy, antonyms....in the social realm, universals include a division of labor, social groups, age grading, the family, kinship systems, ethnocentrism, play, exchange, cooperation, and reciprocity; in the behavioral realm, universals include aggression, gestures, gossip, and facial expressions; in the realm of the mind, universals include emotions, dichotomous thinking, wariness

---

[4] Foley (2001); Powers et al. (2015).

[5] This phrase is commonly associated with Alexandre Dumas (1802–1970) and his novel *The Four Musketeers*, but it has far more ancient origins (e.g., Shakespeare uses this phrase in *The Rape of Lucrece*). In its Latin form (*unus pro omnibus, omnes pro uno*), this phrase has become the unofficial motto of Switzerland.

[6] See Brown (1991), and also related insightful discussions by Levy (2004), Norenzayan (2019), Schatzki (2003), Wierzbicka (2018), and Valsiner (2021).

around or fear of snakes, empathy and psychological defense mechanisms."[7] Brown also lists numerous human universals that are linked to both biology and culture, such as breathing and sexuality.[8] These core human similarities are often overlooked because they seem so obvious, and they are less sexy than the surface-level differences that are so easily noticed and opportunistically flagged.

The same misguided trend of exclusively giving priority to differences is reflected in discussions about (so-called) race in the media, in politics, in everyday life, and also in academic discussions about "racial diversity."[9] These discussions about "race" imply that there are huge genetic differences between groups, and genetic uniformity within groups. But this is a mistaken assumption. As the *American Anthropological Association* has clarified, "…there is greater variation within 'racial' groups than between them."[10] Randomly selected pairs of individuals from the same population tend to be more genetically similar than pairs of individuals from different populations.[11] Studies have replicated the finding that most genetic variation is found within rather than between populations.[12] Thus, *from a scientific perspective, it is human genetic similarities that are striking, not differences.*[13] The way the term "race" is commonly used today is a social construction, a fiction; it is not scientifically real.

Human similarities are like the largest part of the iceberg submerged underwater, but our attention is repeatedly drawn to the much smaller human differences that are clearly visible because they stick out above the water. This book introduces *omniculturalism*, a path for prioritizing and celebrating the vast and deep—but often overlooked—similarities between people, and also giving some (secondary) attention to the easily noticed differences, the tip of the iceberg sticking out above the water. Omniculturalism celebrates the deep similarities that exist between people, and embraces how we humans have far more important commonalities than differences. However, omniculturalism also gives attention to group differences, as a secondary priority.

The omnicultural path leads us to celebrate all the very important characteristics humankind have in common, such as our shared future on the only planet we can inhabit for the foreseeable future. This seems like such a commonsense and noncontroversial approach, yet it goes against current national and international trends.

---

[7] Brown (2004).

[8] Brown (1991, p. 47). The claim that in the realm of language, a universal is "…an inverse ratio between the frequency of use and length of words…" (Brown, 1991, p. 47) does not apply to Mandarin Chinese. Most words in Mandarin Chinese are only one or two syllables, so the length of words has a very limited range.

[9] This includes discussions about "interculturalism," prominent in the United Kindom (Cantle, 2012).

[10] American Anthropological Association (2000).

[11] Bamshad et al. (2004).

[12] Witherspoon et al. (2007).

[13] Of course, there is some benefit to studying genetic differences, such as in the area of health (Bamshad et al., 2004, p. 606).

Everywhere we look, the exaggeration, glorification, and also fabrication of inter-group differences is a much stronger theme than the celebration of human common-alities, even though our similarities run much deeper than our differences. Just look at how differences between groups—including ethnic groups, religious groups, lan-guage groups, and, of course, nationalities—are front and center in all the debates in the media, academia, and everyday life. These intergroup differences, including the fictional ones, are repeatedly used as justification for treating groups differently. You and I are swimming against the prevailing currents when we give priority to human similarities and focus primarily on our common humanity rather than on differences.

Why Is Priority Given to Intergroup Differences?

How is it that we so readily overlook foundational human similarities and give high-est priority to *differences* between groups? The group differences that have become prioritized and celebrated sometimes have a kernel of truth to them, rather like the kernel of truth sometimes found in stereotypes.[14] However, very often the intergroup "differences" that are celebrated are exaggerated and magnified. Later in this book (in Chap. 6), I discuss scientific evidence that shows how there does not have to be real or important differences between groups for us to perceive vast gulfs between them, and also to show bias in favor of the ingroup. We even sometimes justify dev-astating wars and atrocities on the basis of differences between groups that are arbi-trary, fictional, and manufactured. Why is it that from the level of everyday interpersonal social interactions between neighbors and coworkers to the interna-tional level of relations between nation states the focus is on differences between people? A look back at our recent experiences reveals that at the heart of our focus on intergroup differences is the modern concern with *rights*, what we are owed, and the relative neglect of *duties*, what we owe others.[15]

"Women's rights!" "Black rights!" "Gay rights!" We are now in an age of *run-away rights*, when the demand for new rights is hurtling along in new directions.[16] Notice that no group marches under the banner of "duties" and demands "We want our duties!" Everyone in this era loudly declares "We demand our rights!" There have been other historical eras when duties were given highest priority. For exam-ple, in Europe during the Middle Ages, relationships were largely regulated by the duties people had toward one another; the individualistic citizen who focuses on "my rights" gradually emerged after this period.[17] Before then, even the king of England had duties to others which he had to fulfil, as specified in the *Magna Carta*

---

[14] The "kernel of truth" in stereotypes continues to be explored (e.g., see Foo et al., 2022).

[15] See readings in Finkel and Moghaddam (2005).

[16] Moghaddam et al. (2024).

[17] Ullman (1966).

(1215).[18] But there was a gradual decline in the priority given to duties, and a relative rise in the importance given to rights, particularly with widespread industrialization from the eighteenth century.

Industrialization came with a weakening of traditional ties and communities, and increased challenges to the landed gentry who had historically dominated politics. Among the first people to directly and seriously challenge the political power of the traditional landed gentry were entrepreneurs building businesses, as well as people in the emerging new professions such as medicine and law. These new professional groups demanded political rights for the new middle classes. Their demands met with gradual success, as reflected, for example, in the 1832 Parliamentary reforms in England, which gave the vote to men of the new middle classes.[19] In novels such as *Middlemarch* (1872), George Eliot (1819–1880) and other authors present vivid portraits of this shift of power from the traditional landed gentry to the new entrepreneurs, bankers, and professionals, and the priority given to rights rather than duties in the emerging industrial world.[20]

Over the course of the nineteenth and twentieth centuries, the minority groups that (correctly!) rose up to challenge the status quo and try to improve their access to power and resources all demanded equal rights for themselves and sometimes for others as well. Gradually, all white men (even poor ones) in the more progressive countries gained the right to vote in political elections, and from the end of the nineteenth century, democracies began to give the right to vote to women as well (white women in the United States gained the right to vote in 1920, and many countries around the world gave this right to women around the same time[21]). But in practice, ethnic minorities have only been able to enjoy the right to vote since the 1960s, and even now ethnic minorities in the United States and some other countries have to overcome serious hurdles in order to actually cast votes in political elections. Throughout these historical changes, various ethnic, religious, sexual orientation, language, and other types of minorities have been mobilizing for equal rights. In essence, the cultural context in which these minorities have been functioning has led to them to evolve and change to demand more rights. In the twenty-first century, we have entered the age of runaway rights.

A number of consequences, some of them highly positive, have followed the mobilization of minorities and their demand for equal rights. Over the course of this evolution, these minorities have adapted and collectively mobilized to improve the possibility of their success. Part of this adaptation has involved the construction of group identities that emphasize the avowedly different and even unique aspects of each group as compared to other groups. The members of minority groups have engaged in social differentiation, attempting to position their ingroups in vacant spaces, so that their constructed group identities stand out as distinct and different

---

[18] Holt et al. (2015).

[19] This reform came under the threat of radical revolt (Aidt & Franck, 2015).

[20] Eliot (1964).

[21] Sneider (2010).

from the identities of other groups.[22] For example, African Americans creatively redefined their characteristics in positive ways (e.g., "Black is Beautiful") and constructed a unique collective identity that is both positive and different from that of Whites, Hispanics, and other groups. In this way, "universalism" was abandoned, and "being different" was adopted as a path to gaining fuller ethnic rights.[23]

This process of social differentiation and the search for vacant spaces is integral to evolution, and it should be no surprise that it has led to change and adaptation in human groups. Each group adapts in order to increase its access to resources and to improve its survival chances. The outcome is the development of group identities that are positioned as separate, independent, unique. In essence, in the twenty-first-century environment in which groups compete, it is intergroup *differences* not similarities that win vacant spaces and new resources. In this context, groups become motivated to neglect deep human commonalities, but to discover, highlight, exaggerate, and even fabricate new differences between themselves and other groups. I will refer to this as the "in search of group differences movement."

Researchers Search for Intergroup Differences

Another reason for the priority given to differences rather than similarities between groups in contemporary societies is the strong motivation among social science researchers in their competitions with one another to "discover" new intergroup differences.[24] This motivation is associated with the tendency of social science researchers to align themselves with the "in search of group differences movement." In major areas of study such as anthropology and cross-cultural psychology, longer and longer lists are being generated through thousands of studies published each year, showing how groups are different from one another. Almost no attention is given to the fact that the vast majority of intergroup differences shown are relatively less important than the foundational intergroup similarities that characterize humankind. Also, the discovery that some of the seminal cultural-differences studies, such as Margaret Mead's *Coming of Age in Samoa* (1928), present a misleading picture of intergroup differences has had no real impact on the juggernaut of cross-cultural research as it gathers data on intergroup differences while ignoring deeper intergroup similarities.[25]

Psychological science might have provided a remedy to this exclusive focus on intergroup differences and the extreme neglect of human commonalities. After all, psychology is often defined as the science of human behavior, with the goal of

[22] For a discussion of psychological research on social differentiation, see Lee et al. (2008).

[23] Mounk (2023) provides a lively discussion of how the "cancel culture" and left-wing liberalism have contributed to this rejection of universalism.

[24] Brown (1991, 2004) is among the researchers who raise similar points.

[25] There have been serious attempts to try to minimize bias in research on cross-cultural differences (Jones & Donmoyer, 2021).

discovering universals. Unfortunately, psychology has not been able to serve this key corrective function, because the vast majority of psychological studies, even cross-cultural ones, are conducted with student participants from Western societies.[26] The sampling of participants in psychological research is seriously flawed, drawn mainly from Western, educated, industrialized, rich, and democratic (WEIRD) countries.[27] This means that claims about the discovery of universals on the basis of psychological research are highly questionable.

For example, I could quickly gather data for a (supposed) "50-nation psychological study" without even leaving my university office. To carry out such a study, I would electronically send my research instruments and procedures to 50 colleagues in universities in different countries around the world, and ask them to collect data using students in their classes as our study participants. I would speedily have results back from around the world, and I would then analyze and write up my so-called 50-nation study. I could then declare that I have discovered certain cross-cultural differences, based on results across the 50 nations. Of course, the student samples used in my study are not representative of humankind, or even of their own societies (!), and my claim to have discovered cross-cultural differences around the world is nonsense. This kind of "cross-cultural" research with inadequate samples represents one of the ways in which mainstream psychology has failed.[28]

The research procedures and sampling used by anthropologists put them in a relatively better position compared to psychologists to make claims about universals in human behavior. However, anthropologists have themselves helped to strengthen the "in search of group differences movement," and their research is primarily designed to show differences between groups. This is no doubt partly a reaction against the values of colonialism and imperialism and a fear that highlighting and celebrating universals would result in negative reactions from critics of Western dominance. After all, most researchers in anthropology (and almost all other academic fields) are based in Western nations. This raises the question: "is the declaration of what is universal on the basis of anthropological research just another case of Western powers telling non-Westerners that "we are all the same" and defining universals for everybody around the world, but from a Western perspective?" This is a well-founded fear, and reflects some of the thoughtful reactions I have received to the idea of omniculturalism.

---

[26] Moghaddam and Lee (2006).

[27] Henrich et al. (2010).

[28] See chapter 7 in Moghaddam (2023).

Who Defines Humanity and Human Universals?

I have learned from opportunities to debate omniculturalism in live presentations, as well as to explore the idea in publications.[29] During this process, I have been fortunate to receive some extremely insightful critical feedback.[30] After all, omniculturalism gives priority to human "universals," and only secondarily attends to intergroup differences. A major challenge concerns the question: "Who defines humanity and human universals?"

The history of colonialism and imperialism raises serious concerns about this question, because experience shows that groups with more power get more of a say in defining humanity and human universals. For example, in the nineteenth century, the "sun never set on the British empire," and British authorities defined the standards for correct behavior in British colonies that were as culturally different and geographically far apart as India, Australia, and Canada. More broadly, European powers defined the standards for their extensive colonies in the non-Western world; to use Victor Kiernan's phrase, Europeans positioned themselves as *The Lords of Human Kind*.[31] In the twenty-first century, China is leading the charge against "universal values" which it argues are being imposed by Western powers in self-serving ways. A message from critics is "modernization does not equal Westernization."[32]

Within societies as well, there are enormous group-based inequalities in power and resources, so that some groups enjoy far greater influence to define humanity and human universals.[33] For example, in 2019 in the United States, the typical White family had eight times the wealth of the typical Black family and five times the wealth of the typical Hispanic family.[34] Obviously, in this context, Whites have far greater resources to influence how humanity and human universals are defined. Consequently, the question "Who defines humanity and human universals?" is extremely relevant and important, particularly from the perspective of minorities. But it would be a tragic mistake to interpret this to mean that we must reject the idea of universals, and not seek to discover more about what all humans have in common.

Rather than reject universals, we must ensure that universals are accurately identified, and correctly put to use without resulting in bias against some groups and favoritism toward others. The identification and adoption of universals must work in favor of all humankind, and not be biased in favor of a particular group or individual(s). Is this possible to achieve? Are there examples of such universals, identified and put to work for humanity, so that groups with different levels of

---

[29] For journal papers, see Moghaddam (2009, 2012), Moghaddam and Breckenridge (2010). For examples of discussions in books, see Moghaddam (2016, 2019, 2023).

[30] I am particularly grateful for critical commentary from Bilewicz and Bilewicz (2012).

[31] Kiernan (2015).

[32] The Economist (2023, p. 35).

[33] Piketty (2014).

[34] Federal Reserve, https://www.federalreserve.gov/econres/notes/feds-notes/disparities-in-wealth-by-race-and-ethnicity-in-the-2019-survey-of-consumer-finances-20200928.html.

power, influence, and resources all benefit equally? I am the first to admit that we have not achieved this goal. However, we have made valiant efforts that are worth supporting, emulating, and improving upon. One such example is the *United Nations Declaration of Human Rights*, endorsed by almost all members of the United Nations in 1948 (no members opposed).[35]

The *United Nations Declaration of Human Rights* was developed after the Second World War, through meetings held in the United States under the brilliant leadership of Eleanor Roosevelt (1884–1962).[36] Of course, this formulation of human rights can be faulted as not giving enough attention to collective rights, and also for neglecting human duties.[37] The *United Nations Declaration of Human Rights* has been faulted as reflecting a Western and particularly US bias, and also as being hypocritical for applying double standards around the world.[38] That is, those with power are sometimes held to a different human rights standard. However, my contention is that this *Declaration*, despite weaknesses in its content and application, has been beneficial for humankind. The world is better because *United Nations Declaration of Human Rights* has existed.

Can the *United Nations Declaration of Human Rights* be improved upon? Yes, it can and must be improved upon. But just because it is not perfect, does not mean we should abandon efforts to improve upon the work already undertaken and to make further progress toward establishing universals in human rights. Similarly, the *Paris Agreement* which was adopted by almost all of the countries of the world at the *United Nations Climate Change Conference* (COP21) in Paris in 2015 is a valiant effort to establish some basic universal standards for combatting global warming. Again, there are numerous shortcomings to the *Paris Agreement*, and it in some ways reflects power imbalances between high-income and low-income nations around the world, but it is part of a necessary and worthwhile program to establish universal standards in the area of the environment.[39] Indeed, if we do not succeed in establishing and abiding by universal standards in climate change, our collective human future on planet earth is in grave peril.

My argument is that in areas other than climate change, also, our long-term survival depends on us coming to agreement about universal human standards, and successfully addressing the question, "Who defines humanity and human universals?" A clean environment is a universal human need; it is the right of all humans around the world, and the duty of all governments to adopt policies that guarantee this right. Similarly, free speech, the right to an independent judiciary, and at least all the rights listed in the *United Nations Declaration of Human Rights* reflect fundamental human needs. When these basic rights are lacking and basic needs are not

---

[35] https://www.un.org/en/udhrbook/pdf/udhr_booklet_en_web.pdf.

[36] Cook (2019).

[37] For discussion of the psychology of rights and duties, see Finkel and Moghaddam (2005), Moghaddam (2000), and Moghaddam et al. (2000).

[38] Samson (2020).

[39] See discussions in Klein et al. (2017).

met, societies become corrupt and the quality of life in those societies declines. Objective measures clearly show that corruption is highest in countries that are politically more closed and fail to meet basic human rights needs, such as freedom of expression.[40]

The challenges we face in addressing the question "Who defines humanity and human universals?" must not lead us to abandon the quest to define human universals. This is in part because minorities and all those with less power and resources *would suffer most* if we abandon universals, and instead adopt a relativist position.[41] On the surface, relativism benefits minorities, because it allows each group to define morality and justice according to its own criteria—which could be different and even in some respects unique for each group. However, *in practice* relativism on both the global stage and within individual societies enables those with most power and resources to force others to accept their biased and unfair terms and judgements. When there are no universal criteria, whoever has the biggest gun gets to determine what is the law; *might is right* becomes the established norm.

Consider two examples of "might is right," the first international and the second national, which emerge from a relativist position. The *International Criminal Court* (ICC) was established in 1998, when 120 states adopted the *Rome Statue* of the ICC. In an ideal world, the ICC would bring the perpetrators of serious crimes around the globe to justice, irrespective of their nationalities and other group affiliations. The ICC should serve as a court of law for all the world, based on universal-international law. Unfortunately, the United States did not join the ICC. Why? Because the United States does not want to face the possibility of its leaders being prosecuted at the ICC for war crimes. This is a case of the United States taking a relativist position and putting its own national interests ahead of the best interests of humanity and international human rights. As a consequence of this self-serving strategy on the part of the United States and some other powerful nations, in practice only the leaders of relatively weak nations are prosecuted and brought to justice by the ICC.[42]

The second example of "might is right" is from Iran, where after the 1979 anti-shah revolution, the ruling mullahs changed the constitution and laws, so that in many ways Iranian women are now treated as third-class citizens in their own country. Iran has refused to sign on to the *Convention on the Elimination of All Forms of Discrimination Against Women*, adopted by the United Nations General Assembly in 1979. Taking a relativist position, the mullahs argue that they have the right (according to their extremist and severely unjust interpretation of Islam) to reject universal human rights criteria and to implement their own local criteria with respect to women and their (lack of!) fundamental rights in Iran.

---

[40] See the ranking of 180 countries from least to most corrupt https://www.transparency.org/en/cpi/2022/index/deu.

[41] Moghaddam (1992).

[42] See Villa-Vicencio (2009).

The failure of the United States to join the International Criminal Court and the failure of Iran to sign on to the *Convention on the Elimination of All Forms of Discrimination Against Women* both arise from a rejection of universal principles and result in a "might is right" relativist outcome. The United States has the power to resist international pressure to force it to join the ICC, and Iranian mullahs (backed by the guns of the Republican Guards in Iran) have the military power to force Iranian women to conform with their role as third-class citizens in Iran. What is the solution to this situation? Obviously at present in these two instances, the question "Who defines humanity and human universals?" is being answered by those with greater military power. But this is very far from ideal, and I am proposing that we adopt a different approach, one based on giving priority to *human universals* through procedures that involve international bodies, such as the United Nations (UN). Of course, the UN has many faults, but it provides a much better path forward than allowing guns to rule according to a "might is right" approach.

In conclusion, then, I accept that agreeing on human universals is extremely challenging. Our experiences with the *United Nations Declaration of Human Rights*, the *International Criminal Court*, the *Paris Agreement on Climate Change*, and the *Convention on the Elimination of All Forms of Discrimination Against Women* testify to the difficulty of this challenge. However, we should not abandon this universalist path. The alternative path of relativism, of highlighting, manufacturing and celebrating differences between groups, and arguing that the actions of each group can only be judged within its own value system, is detrimental to all humanity, but especially so for women and other minorities. In a world where intergroup differences and relativism take center stage, those with the biggest guns take control and put into practice their own biased and unfair version of justice.

Plan of the Book

Following this introductory chapter, the second chapter explores the global context of diversity and inclusion. Globalization has resulted in enormous and rapid movements of cultural phenomena and people across national boundaries and regions. A great deal of this movement is new, associated with perceived threats, and has resulted in backlash from different groups of people. For example, new forms of electronic communications have enabled cultural phenomena, including images and ideas, to move around the world, sometimes overcoming barriers at national borders. This has heightened feelings of threat, particularly among national and religious conservatives who are motivated to defend their traditional cultures and lifestyles, central to which are gender roles. Two associated processes are, first, the rise of right-wing nationalism and authoritarian strongmen in Western societies and, second, Islamic extremism in many countries where there are large Muslim populations.[43]

Although the number of people moving around the world has not increased in proportion to world population size, there has been a diversification of immigration, and the people arriving in new lands are often seen as being different from the host society.[44] This is largely because the migrants are arriving in their adopted societies (including in Europe, Australia, New Zealand, and North America) in contexts where differences are actively sought out, highlighted, manufactured, and exaggerated. These perceived differences are often in terms of certain cultural and phenotypic characteristics that only reflect surface issues. In this "celebration of differences" context, foundational human similarities are almost completely overlooked. The "celebration of differences" context is encouraging the host population to ask "How are these people different from us?" rather than to prioritize how the newcomers are in so many ways similar to them, and to the rest of humanity.

Another important factor is the far greater speed at which migrants are moving to their adopted lands and the "sudden contact" the host society is experiencing. From the late twentieth century, advanced transportation systems, electronic communications, and a more interconnected economic world market paved the way for the much faster international movement of hundreds of millions of people each year. Of course, humans have always moved from place to place, but historically this movement has been on foot and/or by animal transportation—not by jet planes. This rapid and massive human movement includes millions of refugees, from non-Western to Western countries, such as from the Middle East to Western Europe and from South America to North America. By the early twenty-first century, there was a strong backlash against this "invasion" of dissimilar others, in societies fixated on "celebrating differences." This backlash is associated with the rise of populist right-wing leaders and the adoption of inward-looking nationalist policies, such as Brexit. This is the global context in which assimilation and multiculturalism, the traditional policies for managing diversity, have been functioning—and failing.

The next seven chapters and the *Afterword* are organized in two main parts. The four chapters in Part I present in a global context *assimilation*, where minorities melt into the mainstream culture or all groups melt into one another, and *multiculturalism*, the highlighting, strengthening, sharing, and celebrating of intergroup differences.[45] Assimilation as a policy for managing diversity is presented in Chap. 3. The historic dominance of assimilation policy is described. A few researchers have contrasted multiculturalism only with interculturalism rather than assimilation, but I do not follow this trend of neglecting assimilation because of the historic and

---

[43] Moghaddam (2006, 2019).

[44] Czaika and De Haas (2015).

[45] Of course, patterns of integration other than assimilation and multiculturalism have been discussed (Berry, 1997) and critically assessed (Kunst, 2021; Rudmin, 2003). However, for the sake of this discussion, my focus is on assimilation and multiculturalism, as the main "grand" policies.

global importance of this approach to diversity management.[46] One argument is that globalization trends are in line with assimilation, as global economic pressures force minorities to conform to majority ways of life. Research on "language death" clearly reflects this trend, as more and more minority languages disappear and dominant languages (particularly English) become used by more people around the world.[47] From this perspective, assimilation will continue to take place along with globalization, unless serious and sustained efforts are made to prevent this trend. After presenting assimilation in Chap. 3, I turn to critically assess this approach to managing diversity in Chap. 4, basing the discussion on empirical psychological research, particularly related to the social identity tradition and similarity-attraction studies.

The discussion in Chap. 5 explores how multiculturalism has emerged, not only as a policy for managing diversity but also as an influential global ideology. The emergence of multiculturalism is discussed in relation to the rise of ethnic minority movements. Influenced strongly by the collective movements of the 1960s, multiculturalism is now (incorrectly, I argue) positioned as representing the interests of minorities. In education, as well as in most major government and private sector institutions, multiculturalism has acquired an almost sacred status; it reflects the de facto "politically correct" position to take.

This is followed by a critical reassessment of multiculturalism in Chap. 6. The main shortcomings of multiculturalism include the supposed parity of cultures and ethnicities serving as a distraction from enormous and growing actual wealth disparities and the relative decline of the economically poorest groups; the mistaken treatment of culture as discrete, independent, and stable; the shortcomings of relativism underlying multiculturalism; the questionable assumption that all minorities are motivated to retain and share their heritage cultures; the problematic focus on celebrating intergroup differences, which has also resulted in the manufacture and exaggeration of differences (including fictional ones), fanning the flames of intergroup conflicts; the sidetracking of minorities from the most fruitful paths, especially in the realm of education; and the weak empirical basis for the multiculturalism hypothesis, which assumes that groups that feel confident and secure in their own identities will be open and accepting toward outgroups. The conclusion of this assessment is that multiculturalism is seriously flawed as a policy for managing diversity—it only represents the interests of elites among ethnic minorities and should be abandoned.

In the two chapters in Part II of the book, omniculturalism is described and critically discussed in global context. The main characteristics and the psychological foundations of omniculturalism are discussed in Chap. 7. Socialization and education in support of omniculturalism is in two main stages. First, until the age of about

---

[46] For an example of researchers contrasting multiculturalism with interculturalism rather than assimilation, see Cantle (2012) and Safdar et al. (2023). Taylor (2012) provides a comparative discussion of multiculturalism and interculturalism in the context of Canada, and Quebec in particular.

[47] Moseley (2010).

14 (after the age when the majority of children have passed into Jean Piaget's stage of formal operations, and have also reached an adequately high level of moral development[48]), priority is given to teaching children about human commonalities in response to the question: "What is a human being?" Children learn about the many important ways in which human beings are similar. Second, in their teenage years, in teaching the young, some attention is also given to differences between human groups. Chapter 8 begins by discussing the traditional approach adopted by major religions and political ideologies to achieve human unity. This traditional approach involves conquering other groups: the world will be united and one, only after everyone else has converted to the faith and/or the political ideology of my group. This contrasts with the omnicultural approach to human unity, which argues that human beings *already are* in foundational ways similar to one another. There already is a common human group, to which all humans belong. The change that needs to take place is psychological, shifting from giving priority to and celebrating human differences to giving priority to and celebrating human similarities, which are pervasive and deep.

Finally, in the *Afterword* it is argued that omniculturalism is far more effective than multiculturalism and assimilation, as a global approach to meeting our common human challenges, particularly human-induced climate change.

References

Aidt, T. S., & Franck, R. (2015). Democratization under the threat of revolution: Evidence from the great reform act of 1832. *Econometrica, 83*, 505–547.

American Anthropological Association. (2000). *Amended statement, response to OMB directive 15: Race and ethnic standards for federal statistics and administrative reporting.* https://www.americananthro.org/ConnectWithAAA/Content.aspx?ItemNumber=2583&RDtoken=47501&userID=6944

Bamshad, M., Wooding, S., Salisbury, B. A., & Stephens, J. C. (2004). Deconstructing the relationship between genetics and race. *Nature Reviews/Genetics, 5*, 598–609.

Berry, J. W. (1997). Immigration, acculturation and adaptation. *Applied Psychology: An International Review, 46*, 5–68.

Bilewicz, N., & Bilewicz, A. (2012). Who defines humanity? Psychological and cultural obstacles to omniculturalism. *Culture & Psychology, 18*, 331–344.

Brown, D. E. (1991). *Human universals.* Temple University Press.

Brown, D. E. (2004). Human universals, human nature & human culture. *Daedalus, 133*, 47–54.

Brown, G., & Desforges, C. (2013). *Piaget's theory.* Routledge.

Cantle, T. (2012). *Interculturalism: The new era of cohesion and diversity.* Springer.

Cook, B. W. (2019). *Eleanor Roosevelt: The war years and after.* (Volume Three, 1939–1962). Viking.

---

[48] For Piaget's theory, see Brown and Desforges (2013). The two most important psychological research approaches to moral development are moral foundation theory (see Maxwell & Narvaez, 2013, for discussions of human development and moral foundations theory) and the theory of Lawrence Kohlberg (1963).

Czaika, M., & De Haas, H. (2015). The globalization of migration: Has the world become more migratory? *International Migration Review, 48*(2), 283–323.

Eliot, G. (1964). *Middlemarch.* Signet Classic. First published 1872.

Finkel, N., & Moghaddam, F. M. (Eds.). (2005). *The psychology of rights and duties: Empirical contributions and normative commentaries.* American Psychological Association Press.

Foley, R. A. (2001). Evolutionary perspectives on the origins of human social institutions. *Proceedings of the British Academy, 110,* 171–195.

Foo, Y. Z., Sutherland, C. A. M., Burton, N. S., Nakagawa, S., & Rhodes, G. (2022). Accuracy in facial trustworthiness impressions: Kernel of truth or modern physiognomy? A meta-analysis. *Personality and Social Psychology Bulletin, 48*(11), 1580–1596.

Haeri, S. (2014). *The law of desire: Temporary marriage in Shi'a Iran.* Syracuse University Press. Revised edition.

Henrich, J., Heine, S. J., & Norenzayan, A. (2010). The weirdest people in the world? *Behavioral and Brain Sciences, 33,* 61–135.

Holt, J. C., Garnett, G., & Hudson, J. (2015). *Magna Carta.* Cambridge University Press.

Jones, J. A., & Donmoyer, R. (2021). Improving the trustworthiness/validity of interview data in qualitative nonprofit sector research: The Formative Influences Timeline. *Nonprofit and Voluntary Sector Quarterly, 50,* 889–904.

Kiernan, V. (2015). *The lords of human kind: European attitudes to other cultures in the imperial age.* Zed Books.

Klein, D., Carazo, M. P., Doelle, M., Bulmer, J., & Higham, A. (Eds.). (2017). *The Paris Agreement on climate change: Analysis and commentary.* Oxford University Press.

Kohlberg, L. (1963). Development of children's orientation toward a moral order. *Vita Humana, 6,* 11–36.

Kunst, J. R. (2021). Are we facing a "causality crisis" in acculturation research? The need for a methodological (r)evolution. *International Journal of Intercultural Relations, 85,* A4–A8.

Lee, N., Lessem, E., & Moghaddam, F. M. (2008). Standing out and blending in: Differentiation and conflict. In F. M. Moghaddam, R. Harré, & N. Lee (Eds.), *Global conflict resolution through positioning analysis* (pp. 113–131). Springer.

Levy, N. (2004). Evolutionary psychology, human universals, and the standard social science model. *Biology and Philosophy, 19,* 459–472.

Maxwell, B., & Narvaez, D. (2013). Moral foundations theory and moral development and education. *Journal of Moral Education, 42,* 271–280.

Moghaddam, F. M. (1992). There can be a just and moral social constructionist psychology, but only in a social world that is homogeneous and/or static. In D. N. Robinson (Ed.), *Social discourse and moral judgment* (pp. 167–179). Academic Press.

Moghaddam, F. M. (2000). Toward a cultural theory of human rights. Theory & Psychology, 10, 291–312.

Moghaddam, F. M. (2006). *From the terrorists' point of view: What they experience and why they come to destroy.* Praeger.

Moghaddam, F. M. (2009). Omniculturalism: Policy solutions to fundamentalism in the era of fractured globalization. *Culture & Psychology, 15,* 337–347.

Moghaddam, F. M. (2012). The omnicultural imperative. *Culture & Psychology, 18,* 304–330.

Moghaddam, F. M. (2016). *The psychology of democracy.* American Psychological Association Press.

Moghaddam, F. M. (2019). *Threat to democracy: The appeal of authoritarianism in an age of uncertainty.* American Psychological Association Press.

Moghaddam, F. M. (2023). *How psychologists failed: We neglected the poor and minorities, favored the rich and privileged, and got science wrong.* Cambridge University Press.

Moghaddam, F. M., & Lee, N. (2006). Double reification: The process of universalizing psychology in the Three Worlds. In A. Brock (Ed.), *Internationalizing the history of psychology* (pp. 163–182). New York University Press.

Moghaddam, F. M., & Breckenridge, J. (2010). Homeland security and support for multiculturalism, assimilation, and omniculturalism policies among Americans. *Homeland Security Affairs, 4,* 1–14.

Moghaddam, F. M., Louis, W. R., & Banks, R. (2024). Runaway rights: How rights become expanded, adapted, and coopted. *Culture & Psychology.* https://doi.org/10.1177/1354067X241226457

Moghaddam, F. M., Slocum, N. R., Finkel, N., & Harré, R. (2000). Toward a cultural theory of duties. *Culture & Psychology, 6,* 275–302.

Moseley, C. (Ed.). (2010). *Atlas of the world's languages in danger.* UNESCO.

Mounk, Y. (2023). *The identity trap: A story of ideas and power in our time.* Penguin.

Norenzayan, A. (2019). Why we believe: Religion as a human universal. In H. Høgh-Olesen (Ed.), *Human morality and sociality: Evolutionary and comparative perspectives* (pp. 58–71). Macmillan International. First published 2010.

Picketty, T. (2014). *Capital in the twenty-first century* (Trans. A. Goldhammer). The Belknap Press of Harvard University Press.

Powers, S. T., van Schaik, C. P., & Lehmann, L. (2015). How institutions shaped the last major evolutionary transition to large-scale human societies. *Philosophical Transactions of the Royal Society B, 371,* 20150098.

Rahimzadeh, A. (2020). Fraternal polyandry and land ownership in Kinnaur, Western Himalaya. *Human Ecology, 48,* 573–582.

Rudmin, F. W. (2003). Critical history of the acculturation psychology of assimilation, separation, integration, and marginalization. *Review of General Psychology, 7,* 3–37.

Safdar, S., Chahar Mahali, S., & Scott, C. (2023). A critical review of multiculturalism and interculturalism as integration frameworks: The case of Canada. *International Journal of Intercultural Relations, 93,* 101756.

Samson, C. (2020). *The colonialism of human rights: Ongoing hypocrisies of western liberalism.* Polity Press.

Schatzki, T. R. (2003). Human universals and understanding a different socioculture. *Human Studies, 26,* 1–20.

Sneider, A. (2010). The new suffrage history: Voting rights in international perspective. *History Compass, 8*(7), 692–703.

Taylor, C. (2012). Interculturalism or multiculturalism? *Philosophy and Social Criticism, 38,* 413–423.

The Economist. (2023). *The message to the global south: China tells developing countries that "universal values" are a form of racism.* July 8th, p. 35.

Ullman, W. (1966). *The individual and society in the Middle Ages.* Johns Hopkins University Press.

Valsiner, J. (2021). *General human psychology.* Springer.

Villa-Vicencio, C. (2009). *Walk with us and listen: Political reconciliation in Africa.* Georgetown University Press.

Wierzbicka, A. (2018). I know: A human universal. In S. Stich, M. Mizumoto, & E. McCready (Eds.), *Epistemology for the rest of the world* (pp. 215–250). Oxford University Press.

Witherspoon, D. J., Wooding, S., Rogers, A. R., Marchani, E. E., Watkins, W. S., Batzer, M. A., & Jorde, L. B. (2007). Genetic similarities within and between human populations. *Genetics, 176,* 351–359.

Piketty, T. (2014). Capital in the twenty-first century (Trans. A. Goldhammer). The Belknap Press of Harvard University Press.

Chapter 2
Understanding Diversity and Inclusion in the Context of Fractured Globalization

How should we manage diversity?[1] The process of *globalization*, the increasing interconnectedness and homogeneity of the different societies around the world, suggests that the entire world is the most appropriate context for assessing how we should manage diversity. However, local contexts are suggested as more appropriate by the more recent trend of *deglobalization*, involving a strong and broadly based backlash against "one world" and a move back to localism.[2] Globalization and deglobalization trends are taking place simultaneously, and both have considerable force. This has resulted in competing movements that are on the one hand supportive of further globalization, but on the other hand pushing for deglobalization and localism.[3] At the same time, it would be misguided to ignore the interconnected nature of national and global trends, or what has been referred to as the national nature of globalization, and the global nature of nationalism.[4]

Another feature of the twenty-first-century context for managing diversity and inclusion is the complex relationship between immigration and globalization. The backlash against globalization is in part because of the arrival of millions of immigrants and refugees over a short time period, which has created perceived threats and backlash against minorities among many different host populations around the world. This backlash is associated with anti-globalization and is present in both Western and non-Western countries; it is as clearly evident in South Africa and India, as it is in Western countries such as the United States and the United Kingdom.[5] This perception of immigrants and refugees as threats is also prevalent

---

[1] The issue of diversity management is dealt with in some depth in the business world, with particular focus on the link between diversity and performance (Yadev & Lenka, 2020).

[2] Bello (2004).

[3] Kornprobst and Paul (2021).

[4] Billig (2023).

[5] See the special issue of papers edited by Mansfield et al. (2021).

© The Author(s), under exclusive license to Springer Nature Switzerland AG 2024
F. M. Moghaddam, *The Psychology of Multiculturalism, Assimilation, and Omniculturalism*, SpringerBriefs in Psychology,
https://doi.org/10.1007/978-3-031-62597-8_2

among the poor and economically disadvantaged, who see themselves most directly competing with immigrants for jobs, housing, health, and other basic services.[6]

However, this perceived threat also arises because host populations of all social classes feel that immigrants are a threat to their identities—including their cultures, languages, religions, and ways of life more broadly.[7] In practice, the perceived threat of immigrants and refugees is both material and psychological, with the two being interconnected. Similarly, attitudes toward globalization and immigration are interconnected, as suggested by David Leblang and Margaret Peters, "…The backlash to globalization has increased the salience of immigration for those who oppose it."[8]

Integral to globalization is increased large-scale and rapid movement of people across national boundaries and regions of the world.[9] This population movement is in part because of "push" factors, such as devastating wars, political repression, and harsh economic conditions, particularly in the Near and Middle East, as well as regions of South America and Africa. But according to world population growth trajectories,[10] another powerful factor resulting in population movements is differences in demographic trends in low-income and high-income societies. The world population continues to grow, but this growth is extremely uneven, with some parts of the world (particularly Africa) rapidly increasing population and some other parts (particularly Europe) decreasing in population level.[11] The share of the working age population (aged between 25 and 64 years) has been increasing in most low-income societies, but decreasing in most high-income societies. Europe has an aging and declining population and needs immigration to try to at least maintain population levels.[12]

Africa is the region with the highest population growth, predicted to reach between 2 and 3.1 billion by 2060. Sub-Saharan Africa has the youngest population in the world, and the population growth in Africa is well above the 2.1 "replacement" level.[13] It is the same for much of South America. This higher fertility trend will probably continue until women in these regions routinely benefit from higher number of years of education (this also applies to immigrants—female immigrants to Europe have lower birth rates as they enter higher education[14]). The result of these population growth imbalances is that people move from the low-income societies that have a population "surplus" to the high-income societies that have a population

---

[6] McDermott et al. (2019).

[7] Jetten (2019) provides a social identity theory account of this opposition to immigrants from both low- and high-status individuals.

[8] LeBlang and Peters (2022, p. 385).

[9] De Haas et al. (2019).

[10] See section 6 in Lutz et al. (2019).

[11] United Nations (2022).

[12] For more details of trends in Europe, see Eurostat (2023); Parr (2023).

[13] Kulu et al. (2019).

[14] Kulu et al. (2019).

"deficit." Approximately between 2 and 4 million migrants are needed to move to Europe alone every year, in order to meet labor needs.[15]

I explore this vast population movement from an evolutionary perspective, and in Part I I explain the process of *sudden contact*, "…the swift coming together of life forms with no previous history of contact."[16] Sudden contact has a number of mostly negative consequences for majority-minority relations, with particularly serious implications for societies characterized by diversity. These consequences are discussed in Part I of this chapter. In Part II, I further examine the competing processes of globalization and deglobalization, captured in what I have termed *fractured globalization*, "…the tendency for sociocultural disintegration to pull in a local direction at the same time that macroeconomic and political systems are set up to accelerate globalization."[17] We shall see that fractured globalization involves the psychological need that is strong in many people for local identities, pulling in a direction that is the opposite of movement in macro-level economic and political forces. Thus, after examining the majority-minority relations in an evolutionary context, we look more closely at the competing influence of psychological factors pulling toward the local and economic-political factors pulling in the opposite direction toward the global.

Sudden Contact and Globalization: An Evolutionary Perspective

Throughout evolution, life forms have adapted to their environments, which include life forms that coexist in the same neighborhood. For example, cheetahs evolved their characteristics in relation to both their prey and their competitors for food, such as lions.[18] Other animals who compete for food with lions have also been forced to make adaptations. A study of two populations of spotted hyena in national parks in Kenya showed that the reproductive success of hyenas was directly related to competition for food with lions.[19]

Like the adaptation of cheetahs and hyenas in competition with lions, other life forms also develop survival strategies in relation to their environments. When changes in the environment take place slowly, life forms have more opportunities to make the necessary adaptations to increase their survival chances. For example, when a food source declines, because of disease or other factors, if the decline is gradual and shallow, the life forms dependent on this food source have more opportunities to adapt and find alternative food sources. However, if a major food source

---

[15] Lutz et al. (2019).

[16] Moghaddam (2008, p. 98).

[17] Moghaddam (2008, p. 13).

[18] Broekhuis et al. (2017).

[19] Watts and Holekamp (2008).

disappears suddenly, a life form dependent on this food source has little opportunity to adapt and will very probably suffer a sharp decline in numbers, or even extinction. There are many examples of human population declines as a result of lower food supply over the *Holocene*, roughly the last 12,000 years.[20]

Life forms compete for resources (such as food) and develop defense mechanisms to better adapt to competing life forms in their environments. For example, when they are threatened, some toads and puffer fish swell up in size, so they appear more fearsome and also become more difficult to swallow by predators. Such defense mechanisms typically (but not always) evolve over longer time periods.

However, under certain conditions competitor life forms rapidly move into the territory of native life forms in large numbers, and there is little time for native life forms to adapt. The result is *sudden contact*, when there is too little time for native life forms to develop effective defense mechanisms against the newly arrived life forms. This has been the case with many *invasive species*, non-native life forms that enter into new territories and cause harm, and even extinction, to native life forms. Invasive species can evolve through natural processes, such the accidental transportation of life forms to new territories by floods and other extreme weather events. However, recent increases in invasive species across the globe are mostly part of the massive human footprint.

Invasive species have increased through human activities, and they have now spread across the world.[21] For example, consider the case of two types of snakes that have become invasive species, both accidentally introduced to new territories (probably by humans): the brown tree snake introduced to Guam and the python introduced to Florida, United States.[22] The brown tree snake has no natural predators in Guam, with the result that it has thrived and decimated local animals, particularly birds. Likewise, the python has rapidly multiplied in numbers in many parts of Florida, particularly in the south. The imported python is now causing problems for human inhabitants of Florida and competing with alligators for the role of top predator in the Florida Everglades.[23]

The success of local life forms to compete with invasive species depends on a number of factors. Two of the most important of these are *preadaptiveness*, how prepared "…a life form is in terms of biological and other characteristics for successful evolution in contact with particular other life forms in a given environment."[24] The second important factor is *postcontact adaptation speed*, "…how quickly a life form can adapt, under given environmental conditions, during contact with another life form that is in some way or another their competitor in given environmental conditions (of course, if conditions change, they might no longer be competitors)."[25]

---

[20] Bevan et al. (2017).

[21] Baskin (2002); Capinha et al. (2023).

[22] Baskin (2002).

[23] Pittman et al. (2014).

[24] Moghaddam (2008, p. 96).

[25] Moghaddam (2008, p. 96).

When a local life form comes into contact with an invasive species, but has high preadaptiveness and/or high postcontact adaptation speed, this local life form will probably be less troubled by the invasive species life form. However, if a life form has low preadaptiveness and/or low postcontact adaptation speed during contact with a particular invasive species, then the chances of decline and even extinction are higher.

This is the case in the Florida Everglades where, Stephen Leatherman reports on the impact of pythons as invasive species, "Rapid declines of mammals along with starved alligators…are almost certainly tied to the proliferation of pythons. The numbers of raccoons, which were formerly overabundant, and opossums have dropped by 99%; rabbits have effectively disappeared. Deer and panthers are also being significantly impacted in the Everglades."[26] Are there processes similar to this in the human community? Have some groups of humans acted as "invasive species" and detrimentally impacted other, host groups? The answer, according to historical records, is a definite "yes!"

The history of Western colonial expansion provides many examples of human intergroup interactions that parallel the behavior and impact of invasive species in the animal world. For example, researchers are still debating the exact mechanisms that resulted in a steep decline of Native American populations in post-Columbus America—the questions raised include: "to what extent did government policies deliberately cause declines in Native American populations and to what degree did disease and other factors bring about this decline "accidentally" as an unintended consequence of indigenous-colonial interaction?"[27] But whatever the source of the decline, the rapid disappearance of Native American populations—what Jorge Klor de Alva describes as "…a devastating demographic collapse"[28]—after the arrival of White settlers in America is not disputed.

From the tens of millions of Native Americans living within the boundaries of the present United States in the fifteenth century,[29] only about 220,000 survived in 1910.[30] Similarly, Western colonization and the impact of the slave trade on Africa were devastating: the tens of millions of individuals captured, enslaved, and forcibly wrenched from their lives in Africa resulted in terrible cultural, social, economic, and demographic costs to African communities.[31] Africa has still not recovered from this ordeal; neither have the descendants of slaves living in different parts of the world. There are numerous historical examples, then, of sudden contact between Western colonists and native people resulting in the rapid decline and even

---

[26] Leatherman (2022, pp. 2–4).

[27] For example, see readings in Panich and Gonzalez (2021).

[28] De Alva (2008).

[29] Actual estimates of the total Native American population before the arrival of Western colonists vary considerably; see Josephy Jr (1991), Mann (2006), and Newson (1993).

[30] Josephy Jr (1991).

[31] Lovejoy (1989).

extinction of locals, such as happened in Tasmania, for example.[32] These historical experiences arising out of "sudden contact" have implications for how we can better understand contemporary large-scale rapid movements of populations across national boundaries and entire regions of the world.

Although immigrants and refugees can bring skills and talents that are highly beneficial to the host society,[33] the rapid arrival of large numbers of newcomers can be perceived to be a serious material and psychological threat to host populations. This is particularly so when the newcomers are in important respects dissimilar to the majority group of the host society. Evolutionary psychologists would argue that dissimilarity on the basis of genetic differences is of vital importance and that discrimination against genetically different refugees and immigrants is hardwired.[34] They argue that we are motivated to perpetuate the genes we carry, and this "whispering within" leads us to discriminate against others who we perceive to be carrying competitor genes.[35]

However, as discussed above, there are also explanations of antagonism toward immigrants and refugees on the basis of perceived identity threats. The identity-based arguments appear more persuasive when we take into consideration a serious weakness in the evolutionary psychology argument: the false assumption that phenotype is an accurate indicator of genotype—that host society members can accurately identify the genetic makeup of immigrants and refugees by looking at them. Irrespective of the exact mechanisms we believe underlie the attraction of host society members to immigrants who they see as more similar to themselves, the research evidence demonstrates that this is a strong and universal pattern (I return to this topic later in this chapter).

From the evolutionary perspective I have adopted, the reaction of host majority group members to sudden contact with large numbers of dissimilar others is part of a long-established pattern. The threat perceived by the host majority group is that they will be overtaken and replaced as a group. It is in this context that we can better understand the chant of White American right-wing extremists, "Jews will not replace us!", expressed during the 2017 demonstrations in Charlottesville, Virginia.[36] Jews are the target of neo-Nazi extremists in twenty-first-century Western societies in large part because of conspiratorial theories about how Jews plot to weaken White Christians and take over from them. An implication is that the multicultural incorporation of Jews in the United States and other multicultural countries has not provided a solution to antisemitism.[37]

---

[32] Ryan (1981).

[33] Borjas (2019).

[34] Van den Berghe (1987).

[35] For the basic philosophy behind this movement, see Dawkins (1989) and Wilson (1975).

[36] Winston (2021).

[37] Goldberg (2023) provides an initial analysis of this issue.

Next, we consider how large-scale migrations are on the one hand being pushed by macro-level economic and political factors, but on the other hand resisted by psychological factors.

Managing Diversity in the Context of Fractured Globalization

The concept of fractured globalization captures two competing and contradictory movements, which are subsumed under the umbrellas of globalization and deglobalization. At the same time that macro-level economic and technological factors are pushing humans toward further globalization, unification, and "one world," psychological factors are pulling humans back to the local, to fragmentation and separatism. At the same time that enormous migration is underway around the globe, and national boarders seem to be melting away, there are rising nationalism and extremist movements to repel "outsiders" away from "the homeland." These two competing and very different movements, one pulling toward the global and the other pulling toward the local, set a highly challenging context for policies to manage diversity.

There is also another level of complexity to this situation: it is not enough for us to understand the actual changes taking place and to map them objectively; we must also understand the subjective experiences of the people involved, and these subjective experiences can be very different from objective realities. For example, supporters of Brexit, the exit of the United Kingdom (UK) from the European Union (EU), feel that Brexit has given UK universities the advantage of benefiting from links with the rest of the world, and not being restricted by EU rules and regulations. However, the situation in practice is captured by an objective assessment of UK higher education, demonstrating "…multiple negative effects and no new opportunities after Brexit."[38] But subjectively, supporters of Brexit feel justified despite the negative objective assessment, because they feel that UK universities are now "free" from the rules and regulations of the EU. No matter how many objective assessments point to the negative outcomes of Brexit, at least some Brexit supporters cling to seeing the "advantage" of "taking back our country" and being free from EU rules and regulations (in the meantime, a number of factors, including sport and external threat from Russia, are helping to construct a stronger European identity and higher cohesion within the European Union[39]).

Similarly, there is not always a close correspondence between the characteristics of groups as subjectively perceived by group members themselves, and the characteristics of groups as they actually exist. For example, groups "X" and "Y" might in practice have very similar lifestyles and characteristics, but the members of both

---

[38] Highman et al. (2023).

[39] For the impact of threat from Russia, see Gehring (2021); for the influence of sport, see Finger et al. (2023).

groups might subjectively believe that their groups are very different from one another. Globalization is leading middle-class lifestyles within and between many different countries to become more similar, particularly in the kind of automobiles, electronic equipment, and other goods and services they use. But this convergence in lifestyles is not reflected in convergence in identities—not even within the same society. For example, an African American lawyer may have the same schooling, income, housing, entertainment, hobbies, and lifestyle as a White American lawyer, but she may see herself as being very different from her White colleague. She may see her identity as being very different from their identity.

The power of psychological factors is particularly reflected in the various collective movements for "independence" that have taken place in modern times. In many cases, the independence movements have been based on subjective feelings about identity, rather than objective criteria. The people involved felt the need to break away and form their own independent country, irrespective of objective measures and outcomes. For example, the partitioning of India, to create modern India (1947), Pakistan (1947), and Bangladesh (1971), and the partitioning of Ireland (1921) to create Northern and Southern Ireland were driven in important ways by subjective identity needs of the groups involved (e.g., Hindus and Muslims in India; Catholics and Protestants in Ireland), rather than by objective material criteria of how well the groups would do economically, as independent rather than unified groups.[40]

An important indication of groups attempting to break away from a "home" country is the number of independence referendums held around the world. These referendums are not new; as far back as the fourteenth century, a referendum was held in present-day France to force independence from the Holy Roman Empire.[41] However, there have been increased attempts at breaking away since the Second World War (1939–1945): The number of secession referendums between 1944 and 1989 were 14, and the number between 1991 and 2019 were 43.[42] This is surprising when we consider the global context: the increasing technological and economic integration of countries, on the surface leading us closer and closer to "one world" in terms of material characteristics.

The most important factors strengthening globalization have been economic and technological, particularly increases in digitization associated with internationalization.[43] As Giovanna Magnani and colleagues explained in 2022, "Over the past 40 years, the emergence of digital technologies, the removal of trade and investment barriers, and reductions in transportation costs have dramatically changed the way organizations build up and orchestrate their manufacturing activities at the global level."[44] The internationalization of manufacturing continues, despite some rethinking of outsourcing and offshoring in response to political pressures to bring

---

[40] For discussions of partitions in recent history, see readings in Dubnov and Robson (2019).

[41] Qvortrup (2021).

[42] Qvortrup (2021; Tables 2 & 3).

[43] Bergamaschi et al. (2021).

[44] Magnani et al. (2022, p. 763).

manufacturing back home. Despite the economic nationalism associated with populist movements in the United States and other countries against the outsourcing of jobs and investments, research and development are becoming more international, as are service industries in areas such as healthcare.[45] For example, tens of millions of consumers go across national borders each year to seek medical care as part of "medical tourism." Hospital chains based in different countries (including, perhaps surprisingly, Turkey) are now offering services internationally.[46]

A clear indication of globalization and greater assimilation at the international level is found through research reporting on language death and a marked decline in the world's language diversity. It is estimated that about 15,000 languages existed in the world when Columbus arrived in North America, but there are only about 6000–7000 languages left today.[47] Nearly 50% of the languages in existence are endangered, and languages are being lost at a rate of 1–3 a month. With the death of languages, we lose traditional knowledge and ways of doing things, such as reckoning time. In *When Languages Die*, David Harrison notes that "Traces of earlier time-reckoning techniques may still be found in many small and endangered languages."[48] Of course, it could be argued that there are developing new forms of English and other dominant languages (e.g., Black English, Hispanic English, and so on), but this does not negate the reality that many traditional languages have disappeared, and many others are endangered and about to become extinct. An extensive study of 6511 living languages showed that the most important predictor of language decline is the number of people who speak the language, and there are hundreds of languages with only a small number of speakers left.[49]

Returning to our discussion at the start of this chapter, English and other dominant languages can be interpreted as invasive species, rapidly moving into a region and endangering local languages. In line with this interpretation, one of the factors found to predict language decline is road density in a region: more roads enable greater contact with other people who speak a dominant language, which in turn leads to a decline in local "minority" languages.[50] Given the important role language has in sustaining group culture, the loss of languages is also associated with a decline in cultural diversity.

But, again, we should not assume that a decline in differences between groups on the basis of objective measures will necessarily correspond with how group members subjectively perceive the differences between their groups. Groups "X" and "Y" might be very similar to one another on objective measures, but still perceive their groups to be vastly different from one another. Subjective perceptions of group

---

[45] For internationalization of services, see Rammal et al. (2022); for research and development internationalization trends, see Dachs and Zahradnik (2022).

[46] Uner et al. (2020).

[47] Bromham et al. (2022); Crystal (2000).

[48] Harrison (2007, p. 61).

[49] Bromham et al. (2022).

[50] Bromham et al. (2022).

characteristics and intergroup differences can be based on social constructions and fictions about groups that are divorced from reality, but they can still serve as the most important drivers of the behavior of group members.

Concluding Comment

Economic and technological factors are shrinking our world and leading to greater similarities, at least in our material lives. The products and technologies surrounding us are more and more similar. In this sense, globalization forces are in line with assimilations and one world. On the other hand, separatism and independence movements are taking us back to the local, and rejecting pressures for us to melt into one world.

The drive to the local is shaped by psychological experiences and identity motivations and needs. This is reflected as much in Islamic fundamentalists rejecting Westernization and committed to driving Westerners out of Islamic lands, as it is in White nationalists in Western societies rejecting new migrants from South America, Africa, and Asia. These collective movements are based on identity needs and subjective perceptions of intergroup differences. Two groups may be influenced by globalization forces to be objectively very similar, at the same time that they are subjectively perceived by group members as very different.

Globalization is fundamentally changing the broad context of all our lives. Like it or not, we now live in an increasingly interconnected world, with the production of many basic goods being highly dependent on international networks and supply chains.[51] Globalization is in practice largely (but not exclusively) a homogenizing force, pushing human lifestyles in different societies to become more similar. But globalization has been criticized for taking place according to a liberal order.[52] Criticism has come not only from China, Russia, and other dictatorships outside the Western world but also from authoritarian strongmen, extremist nationalists, and populist movements within Western societies. Efforts to push forward a deglobalization agenda are backed by a diversity of forces and are bringing about uncertainty, tensions, and conflicts. The discussion of these issues in Chap. 2 has set the stage for examinations of assimilation and multiculturalism in the four chapters in Part I.

---

[51] Coe and Young (2015).

[52] Paul (2021).

References

Baskin, Y. (2002). *A plague of rats and rubber vines*. Island Press.

Bello, E. (2004). *Deglobalization: Ideas for a new world economy*. Zed Books.

Bergamaschi, M., Bettinelli, C., Lissana, E., & Picone, P. M. (2021). Past, ongoing, and future debate on the interplay between internationalization and digitization. *Journal of Management and Governance, 25*, 983–1032.

Bevan, A., Colledge, S., Fuller, D., Fyfe, R., Shennan, S., & Stevens, C. (2017). Holocene fluctuations in human population demonstrates repeated links to food production and climate. *Proceedings of the National Academy of Sciences, 114*, E10524–E10531.

Billig, M. (2023). The national nature of globalization and the global nature of nationalism: Historically and methodologically entangled. *Theory & Psychology, 33*, 175–192.

Borjas, G. J. (2019). Immigration and economic growth. *National Bureau of Economic Research*, Working Paper 25836. http://www.nber.org/papers/w25836

Broekhuis, F., Thuo, D., & Hayward, M. W. (2017). Feeding ecology of cheetahs in the Maasai Mara, Kenya and the potential for intra- and interspecies competition. *Journal of Zoology, 304*, 65–72.

Bromham, L., Dinnage, R., Skirgard, H., Ritchie, A., Cardillo, M., Meakins, F., Greenhill, S., & Hua, X. (2022). Global predictors of language endangerment and the future of linguistic diversity. *Nature: Ecology & Evolution, 6*, 163–173.

Capinha, C., Essl, F., Porto, M., & Seebens, H. (2023). The worldwide networks of spread of recorded alien species. *Proceedings of the National Academy of Sciences, 120*, e2201911120.

Coe, N. M., & Young, H. W. C. (2015). *Global production networks: Theorizing economic development in an interconnected world*. Oxford University Press.

Crystal, D. (2000). *Language death*. Cambridge University Press.

Dachs, B., & Zahradnik, G. (2022). From few to many: Main trends in the internationalization of business R&D. *Transnational Corporations Journal, 29*, 107–134.

Dawkins, R. (1989). *The selfish gene* (2nd ed.). Oxford University Press.

De Alva, J. J. K. (2008). Colonialism and postcolonialism as (Latin) American mirages. *Colonial Latin American Review, 1*, 3–23.

De Haas, H., Czaika, M., Flahaux, M. L., Mehandra, E., Natter, K., Vezzoli, S., & Villares-Verela, M. (2019). International migration: Trends, determinants, and policy effects. *Population and Development Review, 45*, 885–922.

Dubnov, A. M., & Robson, L. (Eds.). (2019). *Partitions: A transnational history of twentieth-century territorial separatism*. Stanford University Press.

Eurostat. (2023). *Online database*. Retrieved Nov 1, 2023. https://ec.europa.eu/eurostat/data/database

Finger, T., Amann, J., Biel, J., Neimann, A., & Reinke, V. (2023). Researching football, identity and cohesion in Europe. *Sports Law, Policy & Diplomacy Journal, 1*, 131–157.

Gehring, K. (2021). Can external threat foster a European Union identity? Evidence from Russia's invasion of Ukraine. *The Economic Journal, 132*, 1489–1516.

Goldberg, C. A. (2023). From multiculturalism to antisemitism? Revisiting the Jewish question in America. *American Journal of Cultural Sociology*, 1–24.

Harrison, K. D. (2007). *When languages die: The extinction of the world's languages and the erosion of human knowledge*. Oxford University Press.

Highman, L., Marginson, S., & Papatsiba, V. (2023). Higher education and research: Multiple negative effects and no new opportunities after Brexit. *Contemporary Social Science, 18*, 216–234.

Jetten, J. (2019). The wealth paradox: Prosperity and opposition to immigration. *European Journal of Social Psychology, 49*, 1097–1113.

Josephy, A. M., Jr. (1991). *The Indian heritage of America*. Houghton-Mifflin.

Kornprobst, M., & Paul, T. V. (2021). Globalization, deglobalization and the liberal international order. *International Affairs, 97*, 1305–1316.

Kulu, H., Milewski, N., Hannemann, T., & Mikolai, J. (2019). A decade of life-course research on fertility of immigrants and their descendants in Europe. *Demographic Research, 40,* 1345 1374.

Leatherman, S. P. (2022). Management of invasive snakes in coastal environments: A baseline assessment of the Burmese python invasion in the Florida Everglades. *Marine Pollution Bulletin, 182.* https://doi.org/10.1016/j.marpolbul.2022.113996

Leblang, D., & Peters, M. E. (2022). Immigration and globalization (can deglobalization). *Annual Review of Political Science, 25,* 377–399.

Lovejoy, P. E. (1989). The impact of the African slave trade on Africa. *The Journal of African History, 30,* 365–394.

Lutz, W., Amran, G., Bélanger, A., Conte, A., Gailey, N., Ghio, D., et al. (2019). *Demographic scenarios for the EU: Migration, population and education.* Publications Office of the European Union.

Magnani, G., Denicolai, S., & Petersen, B. (2022). Internationalization, value-chain configuration, and the adoption of additive manufacturing technologies. *Industrial and Corporate Change, 31,* 762–782.

Mann, C. C. (2006). *1491: New revelations of the Americas before Columbus.* Knopf.

Mansfield, E. D., Milner, H. V., & Rudra, N. (2021). The globalization backlash: Exploring new perspectives. *Comparative Political Studies, 54,* 2267–2285.

McDermott, M., Knowles, E. D., & Richeson, J. A. (2019). Class perceptions and attitudes toward immigration and race among working-class whites. *Analysis of Social Issues and Public Policy, 19,* 349–380.

Moghaddam, F. M. (2008). *How globalization spurs terrorism: The lopsided benefits of "one world" and why that fuels violence.* Praeger.

Newson, L. A. (1993). The demographic collapse of Native People in the Americas, 1492–1650. *Proceedings of the British Academy, 81,* 247–288.

Panich, L. M., & Gonzalez, S. L. (Eds.). (2021). *Routledge handbook of the archeology of indigenous-colonial interaction in the Americas.* Routledge.

Paul, T. V. (2021). Globalization, deglobalization and reglobalization: Adapting liberal international order. *International Affairs, 97,* 1599–1620.

Parr, N. (2023). Immigration and the prospects for long-run population decreases in European countries. *Vienna Yearbook of Population Research, 21,* 1–29.

Pittman, S. E., Hart, K. M., Cherkiss, M. S., Snow, R. W., Fujisaki, I., Smith, B. J., et al. (2014). Homing of invasive Burmese pythons in South Florida: Evidence for map and compass senses in snakes. *Biology Letters, 10*(3), 20140040.

Qvortrup, M. (2021). Referendums, democracy and separatism. *Review of Nationalities, 10,* 1–13.

Rammal, H. G., Rose, E. L., Ghauri, P. N., Ørberg Jensen, P. D., Kipping, M., Peterson, B., & Scerri, M. (2022). Economic nationalism and internationalization of services: Review and research agenda. *Journal of World Business, 57,* 101314.

Ryan, L. (1981). *The Aboriginal Tasmanians.* University of Queensland Press.

United Nations. (2022). *World population prospects.* United Nations Population Division. https://population.un.org/wpp/Publications/

Uner, M. M., Cetin, B., & Cavusgil, S. T. (2020). On the internationalization of Turkish hospital chains: A dynamic capabilities perspective. *International Business Review, 29,* 101693.

Van den Berghe, P. (1987). *The ethnic phenomenon.* Praeger.

Watts, H. E., & Holekamp, K. E. (2008). Interspecific competition influences reproduction in spotted hyenas. *Journal of Zoology, 276,* 402–410.

Wilson, E. O. (1975). *Sociobiology: The new synthesis.* Harvard University.

Winston, A. S. (2021). "Jews will not replace us!". Antisemitism, inbreeding and immigration in historical context. *American Jewish History, 105,* 1–24. https://muse.jhu.edu/article/804146/pdf

Yadev, S., & Lenka, U. (2020). Diversity management: A systematic review. *Equality, Diversity, and Inclusion: An International Journal, 39,* 901–929.

Part I
Traditional Approaches to Managing Diversity in Global Context

The four chapters in this Part present and critically assess assimilation and multiculturalism, the two main traditional approaches adopted by different societies to manage diversity. Assimilation has been the historically dominant approach, and is in many respects more in line with material trends integral to globalization. Notwithstanding attempts at deglobalization, globalization has acted as a powerful force toward the greater and greater economic and cultural integration of nations around the world. In practice, electronic communications, global mass media, the enormous rise in mass produced and globally available consumer products, the homogenization of education, and entertainment systems, among other things, have resulted in the lifestyles across ethnic groups, nations, and geographical regions, becoming more similar in key respects. However, both globalization and assimilation, as attempted in countries such as France, have resulted in serious backlash. This backlash has involved a variety of different forces in Western societies. On the one hand, it has involved authoritarian strongmen leading populist movements to close national borders and re-prioritize, re-claim, and defend what they see to be their authentic "White Christian national identity." On the other hand, backlash against assimilation has come from ethnic minorities who often feel that they experience exclusion and that their best path forward is to defend their (actual and symbolic) distinct identities and cultures.

Particularly since the 1960s, multiculturalism has been championed as a policy that helps ethnic minorities, and in the twenty-first-century multiculturalism has become dominant in education and most other sectors in many Western and some non-Western societies. The influence of multiculturalism in schools, universities, business and government organizations, and many other domains can be seen especially through the emphasis on the "celebration of differences," and each ethnic group (supposedly) having some special or even unique characteristics. Underlying multiculturalism is relativism, and the focus on all cultures, ethnic groups, and their ways of life being of equal value. Integral to cultural relativism is the idea that the actions of each group can only be evaluated within the value system of the group itself. This perspective is critically assessed and found wanting. I argue that despite the serious difficulties we face on the universalist path, this is the best path for humankind. We must give highest priority to establishing and applying human universals, as discussed in Chap. 1.

Chapter 3
Presenting Assimilation

The goal of this chapter is to present the diversity management policy of *assimilation*, the transformation of different groups to become increasingly similar to one another so that the whole community, whether it be a neighborhood, a city, a nation, or the entire world, becomes homogeneous, cohesive, and better mobilized to achieve its collective goals. Globalization has been accompanied by many different visions and discussions of world citizenship and the idea expressed by Ibrahim Kurt that humankind is becoming "…a big world family."[1] The ideal that all humankind should become one world, one people, with one common identity, culture, and language, has been associated with utopian thinking throughout human history—including the Marxist idea of all the world ultimately becoming one classless society, and the capitalist idea of the world becoming one giant borderless free-market.

In historically immigrant-receiving societies, such as those of North America, Australia, and New Zealand, assimilation has been *in practice* the dominant approach. But at least in research and theoretical discussions, by the middle of the twentieth century, assimilation was pushed aside as support increased for *integration*, the incorporation of migrants into the social, cultural, economic, political, and other major dimensions of the host society, through processes of multidirectional influence.[2] A major criticism of assimilation has been that it neglects the influence that immigrants have on the host society. In addition, critics pointed out that the host society is not homogenous, but already has some level of diversity when new immigrants arrive.

However, I argue that in practice there are different types of assimilation. Rather than dismiss assimilation and adopt integration as the main concept for analyzing minority-majority relations in immigrant-receiving societies, we should take into

---

[1] Kurt (2023).

[2] See discussions in Garcés-Mascareñas and Penninx (2016).

© The Author(s), under exclusive license to Springer Nature Switzerland AG 2024
F. M. Moghaddam, *The Psychology of Multiculturalism, Assimilation,*
and Omniculturalism, SpringerBriefs in Psychology,
https://doi.org/10.1007/978-3-031-62597-8_3

consideration variations in assimilation that actually encompass integration. Specifically, consider the concept of *melting-pot assimilation*, involving the emergence of a new culture through the merging of minority and majority groups.[3] This type of assimilation incorporates multidirectional influence and encompasses an important part of what most of the critics claim has been missing from the concept of assimilation.

One could argue that at the international level, powerful economic and technological forces integral to globalization are actually making assimilation inevitable. These forces are so powerful that they even break down strong national barriers, as Edward Uzoma Ezedike argues from an African perspective, "Globalization entrenches a systemic breakdown of cultural barriers and encourages the assimilation of values from other cultures. Globalization is virtually opposed to nationalism which seeks to protect the interest of an individual nation or culture."[4] The power of globalization derives from not only economic pressures and interdependencies but also the pervasive reach and influence of rapidly advancing electronic communications. Dictatorial regimes such as those ruling Iran and Russia attempt to severely limit the information available to ordinary people via electronic communications, but this comes at a high economic cost to themselves and is not fully successful. After all, when a government limits electronic communications for a large segment of the population (i.e., the non-elite), this also prevents the economy from reaching its potential.

Reactions against globalization have grown, and given the association between assimilation and globalization, it might be assumed that assimilation is also on the wane. However, the impact of globalization (and the associated trend of assimilation) continues to be extensive and deep. This is despite the recent reactions against globalization, partly brought about by the Great Recession of 2008 and the coronavirus (COVID-19) pandemic of 2020–2023. These setbacks highlighted problems that can arise, such as supply-chain breakdowns and bottlenecks in global transportation and communications networks, as a result of rapid market-driven economic integration and the greater interdependence of nations on one another and on international networks.[5] Despite these setbacks, globalization continues to advance, as does assimilation at national and international levels.

Next, I review varieties of assimilation, and some benefits associated with each type. These benefits are substantial and in line with some idealistic visions of how society should develop.

---

[3] Moghaddam (1998, p. 499; 2008, p. 132).

[4] Ezedike (2019, p. 15).

[5] Kobrin (2020).

Varieties of Assimilation

Although the outcome of assimilation is always greater similarity of people, including singularity in their identity, there are different paths for reaching this end. Below, I distinguish between two main paths.

Minority Assimilation

The classic model of assimilation involves minority assimilation: after arriving in the adopted land, minority group immigrants (consciously and unconsciously) change to become more and more similar to the majority group of their host society. This is the classic model of immigrant assimilation outlined by the Chicago School of Sociology early in the twentieth century.[6] According to this model, first-generation immigrants settle in densely populated urban centers and ghettos, where the cost of living is lower, public transportation is available, and immigrants can have access to the kinds of entry-level jobs traditionally open to them. Within a generation or two, the children of these immigrants have made some progress (particularly through education), accessed better-paying jobs, and gradually moved to live in the suburbs where there is better housing, schools, and health services.

Minority assimilation involves one-sided change: minority groups embarking on a journey to become more similar to the majority group of the host society. This includes in the area of language, whereby immigrants adopt the language of the majority group. For example, in the United States, Australia, New Zealand, and the United Kingdom, first-generation immigrants learn English, and the second- and third-generation immigrants become fully fluent in English, and typically beyond the third generation, they abandon their heritage languages.[7] This trend is clear and persistent, despite the misplaced fears of some host society members that new immigrants are refusing to learn English[8] (the language situation in the United States is particularly challenging, because there is no official national language; the Founding Fathers saw no need to establish one. Sharp increases in the Hispanic population since the late twentieth century have resulted in perceived threats from some English speakers, and a vibrant "English-only" movement intent on achieving an "English-only" America[9]).

As I discuss in further detail below, under "benefits of assimilation," minority assimilation has the advantage of moving society toward a clear and unified vision of collective identity. The majority group culture and identity are adopted as an ideal that everyone has to take on, irrespective of where they come from and what

---

[6] Park (1950); Park and Burgess (1921).

[7] Carreira and Kagan (2011, p. 42).

[8] Hinton (1999).

[9] Borden (2014).

their heritage cultures and languages are. But this is not the only kind of assimilation, as I discuss below.

Melting-Pot Assimilation

According to melting-pot assimilation, both minority and majority groups "melt together," and the fusion results in a new society, with a new culture. This is in line with the "new America" that was popularized by Israel Zangwill's play *The Melting Pot*, first performed in 1908.[10] American society would become transformed as new groups of immigrants arrive and add new ingredients to the American melting pot, with their various cultures, languages, values, and lifestyles. These changes would take place alongside shifts in the ever-changing American frontier, with the challenging conditions of frontier life forcing people to adapt, abandon old ways, and take on alternative "American" ways of life. The ever-moving American frontier gives shape to both the new American society and the new Americans, the individual members of that society.[11]

Melting-pot assimilation also assumes that there will be changes in the languages used in the host society, as new groups of immigrants arrive with their many different heritage languages. First, heritage languages would survive for a time, at least among first- and second-generation immigrants. In cases where there are large enough numbers of particular language groups, the immigrant language could survive and become part of the American mosaic. Second, immigrants would not just learn the language of the adopted land as it is spoken by the majority group but also make this language their own, and in some ways change it. For example, consider the way English has adapted as it has been learned and used by different groups of people. At the global level, there are now different "world Englishes."[12]

At the national level, the highly uneven geographical distribution of minorities across countries and across cities helps the retention of heritage languages, as well as the development of new forms of the national language. After they arrive, immigrants do not disperse randomly across the adopted nation. Rather, many immigrants tend to concentrate in *ethnic economic enclaves*, geographical areas with concentrated ethnic economic activity, as well as concentration of ethnic culture and language—two examples are Chinatown and Little Italy.[13] These enclaves provide heritage cultures and languages a supportive foundation. Second, the ethnic economic enclaves also support the development of alternative forms of the majority languages—for example, the many Englishes that are alive in North America. In

---

[10]Zangwill (1909).

[11]Turner (1920).

[12]Melchers et al. (2019).

[13]Portes and Manning (2019).

response to the criticism that there is only one English, the writer James Baldwin asks, "If Black English isn't a language, then tell me what is?"[14]

Forces Pushing Societies and the World Toward Assimilation

From a realist perspective, it can be argued that both minority-assimilation and melting-pot assimilation are underway in tandem around the world, making assimilation inevitable *in practice*. That is, although minority and majority groups often make claims about their differentness and even uniqueness, in practice all groups are becoming more and more similar. The path to increasing similarity across nations and across the world is shaped first and foremost by unstoppable economic and technological forces. These forces are leading to more and more similarity in what I have called hardwiring outside individuals, "...the total way of life of human beings, including the built environment, societal organization, and formal institutions, as well as the informal culture, narratives and all forms of communications, leader-follower relations, and cultural carriers."[15]

The march toward greater and greater similarity in how people in different nations and groups *actually behave*, rather than how they claim to be different, is led by the elite and by the young. The elite around the world are in important ways shaped by exclusive schools and universities that have been modeled after leading Western institutions and follow a similar curriculum. Again, this is an area where we need to distinguish between rhetoric and reality, between political slogans and actual practices. For example, political slogans would have us believe that the universities of Russia, Iran, and China are very different from Western and particularly US universities. But when we get past the political rhetoric, we find that the leading universities of Russia, Iran, and China model themselves after Western universities and educate their students in very similar ways. This is in part because of the international nature of science; after all, physics, chemistry, and other sciences are the same around the world. But it is also because the structure and organization of twenty-first-century universities around the world are modeled after Western and particularly American universities. The similarity in university education is why many graduates from universities in Russia, Iran, China, and other "anti-Western" countries find it so easy to join the brain drain and move to the West. Their education prepares them for life and work in the West.

Young people make enormous contributions to assimilation. This youth-led assimilation has been accelerated and accentuated by electronic communications, which the young were born into and find natural. When we ask, what are the young around the world assimilating into? There are multiple answers, including radical Islam and environmentalism. However, by far the most powerful and widely

---

[14] Baldwin (1997).
[15] Moghaddam (2023a, p. 16).

influential attraction is youth culture in America. From the classic rock and roll of the 1950s to the gangster rap of the twenty-first century, the music, films, and popular youth culture of America is the main global magnet. This is what is influencing most youth around the world, leading them to become more similar, more assimilated into a common global culture.

I have been reminded of the magnetic pull of American youth culture even in contexts where people are avowedly anti-American. During my international work over the last four decades, I have sometimes found myself in contexts where people are demonstrating against the United States and even shouting "Death to America." However, sometimes in these situations when a young person learns that I work in the United States, their response is, "I want to study in America. Can you help me get a visa to go there?" The attraction of American youth culture has created dilemmas for anti-American governments, as they push to establish independent identities and resist assimilation into "one world."

National governments have taken up a variety of positions in relation to assimilation. At the one extreme, a number of countries have struggled to develop a distinct and different anti-Western culture, and to not assimilate into a global culture (which they see as Western dominated). Islamic countries and communist countries are primary examples of this. As part of their fight against assimilation into Western culture, some Islamic and Communist governments are also fighting against the spread of English as an international language and the US dollar as the dominant international currency. At the same time, some of these same governments have attempted to stamp out local cultures and languages within their own national borders, and to achieve assimilation at the national level. For example, in Islamic societies such as Saudi Arabia and Iran, there has been an attempt to establish the same brand of Islam throughout the nation, and to stamp out tribal and ethnic differences.

Some Benefits of Assimilation

Assimilation is associated with a number of important benefits for society, and these arise from the psychological foundations of assimilation. I discuss these below.

Similarity-Attraction and Trust

The most obvious implication of assimilation is that minority and majority groups become more similar to one another. For example, they develop to be more similar in terms of culture and language, as well as core values and norms. They also become more similar in adopting a common, shared identity (a topic that is discussed in more detail later in this chapter). Irrespective of whether this outcome is achieved through minority assimilation or melting-pot assimilation, the end result is greater similarity between people in society. From a psychological perspective, this has important implications, because research clearly shows that greater similarity results in increased attraction. An extensive meta-analysis of research studies suggests that perceived similarity is even more important than actual similarity: the belief in similarity can have a powerful influence, even when similarity is fictional and does not exist in practice (a meta-analysis provides assessments of general trends in research, arrived at through combining and integrating the results of hundreds of different studies).[16]

The link between similarity and attraction is as close as we can get to a universal in social behavior. Extensive research shows that similarity leads to attraction at the interpersonal level.[17] This is true in friendship, and especially so in romantic relationships.[18] Dating agencies work on the basis of similarity-attraction: they try to arrange meetings between individuals who have been identified as being similar on key criteria, in the knowledge that similarity will lead to attraction. Of course, similarity that serves to bring couples together can be on a distinct and even idiosyncratic basis, making a couple very different from most others in their society. For example, devotion to an extreme form of gangster rap might serve as the key similarity between two individuals, and on this characteristic they might be different from others around them.

At the intergroup level, also, evidence demonstrates that people are attracted to the members of outgroups that they see to be more similar. A study that included Algerian-Canadian, English-Canadian, French-Canadian, Greek-Canadian, Jewish-Canadian, and Indian-Canadian samples showed a consistent pattern: the more individuals saw the outgroup as similar to their ingroup, the more they were motivated to have closer relationships with the members of that outgroup.[19] Other studies have shown that in addition to similarity playing an important role in relationships between ethnic groups, similarity-attraction is also a powerful force in relations between religious and political groups.[20] This is in line with research showing that different outgroups are viewed differently,[21] with similarity being a key determinant of which groups are preferred for contact. We prefer similar others partly because they affirm our worldview and show us to be correct.[22]

Another possible benefit of assimilation arises from the relationship between similarity and trust. Researchers have identified a problematic trend, whereby increased ethnic diversity is associated with lower trust among the members of

---

[16] Montoya et al. (2008).

[17] Byrne (1971); Montoya et al. (2008).

[18] Berscheid and Reis (1998).

[19] Osbeck et al. (1997).

[20] Salas-Schweikart et al. (under review).

[21] Zou and Cheryan (2017).

[22] Montoya and Horton (2012) provide a fuller discussion of the processes underlying similarity-attraction, based on an extensive meta-analysis.

society.[23] Given that societies are becoming increasingly diverse, if current trends continue, then trust levels will probably decline even further in the future. One possible solution is suggested by research showing that people are more trusting toward others who they see as more similar to them in values (such as in politics and religion) and group identity.[24] From this perspective, assimilation policy could result in greater similarity between people in society, and this could lead to higher trust levels.

Contact and Improved Intergroup Relationships

Assimilation increases the probability of contact between the members of different minority and majority groups. Contact theory proposes that intergroup relations are improved through contact, an idea that has a long history.[25] It was Gordon Allport (1897–1967) who first formalized contact theory and postulated the conditions in which contact would improve intergroup relations.[26] This is vitally important, because there are many conditions in which the members of different groups have extensive contact with one another, but such contact does not improve their relationships—at least from the perspective of the minority group. I elaborate on this point in the next chapter (Chap. 4).

Allport postulated that contact would only improve relations between groups if four conditions are met in the context in which contact takes place. The two groups should, first, enjoy equal status; second, be in a cooperative rather than a competitive relationship; third, share common goals; and, fourth, have intergroup contact in a community that sanctions and supports such contact. In practice, these four conditions are difficult to achieve, a topic discussed in the next chapter.

Since Allport's foundational contributions, research on intergroup contact has become more optimistic in the possibilities of moving from contact to improved intergroup relations.[27] This optimism has arisen in part through examinations of broad trends in hundreds of research studies on intergroup contact.[28] This new research trend has been used to propose that contact can have beneficial outcomes for intergroup relations *irrespective* of the conditions. This is a sharp contrast from the conclusion of earlier researchers that for intergroup relations to improve, "contact is not enough."[29]

---

[23] Dinesen et al. (2020).

[24] Foddy et al. (2009); Tan and Vogel (2008).

[25] Dovidio et al. (2003, pp. 6–7).

[26] Allport (1954).

[27] Pettigrew (2021).

[28] For example, Pettigrew and Tropp (2006).

[29] Hewstone and Brown (1986).

On the basis of the more optimistic research outlook in the twenty-first century, three types of positive outcomes have been identified from intergroup contact.[30] The first outcome is a *primary transfer effect*, when contact with an individual outgroup member leads to improved attitudes toward the encountered individual and this is generalized to the entire outgroup. A *secondary transfer effect* takes place when a positive interaction with an outgroup individual leads to more favorable views of not just the outgroup represented by the individual but to all outgroups. Finally, the claim has been made that intergroup contact leads to a *tertiary transfer effect*, involving so-called cognitive liberalization, more flexible thinking, and better problem-solving. These are optimistic predictions about the consequences of intergroup contact, independent of the conditions and context of contact.

Meritocracy and Inclusiveness

The United States is often described by its admirers as a "land of opportunity," a place where anyone can make it—as long as they have the drive, talent, and other individual characteristics necessary for success. In the ideal, then, the United States is a meritocracy, a place where the progress achieved by individuals is determined by their personal talents and hard work. Supporters of this image of America point to Barack Obama, Oprah Winfrey, Bill Clinton, Kamala Harris, Ronald Reagan, and many others who began "at the bottom" but managed to attain high status. But this kind of "rags to riches" story can only become reality, it is argued, through a policy of assimilation.

Supporters contend that through assimilation, minority group individuals become more similar to the majority group members, and this enables them to melt into the mainstream and compete on a level playing field. For example, in a society where English is the majority language, minority children can better compete in school when they master English as their first language. Also, by immersing themselves in the mainstream culture, ethnic minority children will be able to compete better on standardized tests. After all, these standardized tests are constantly criticized for (apparently) being culturally biased in favor of the majority group. If this is so, then by becoming immersed in mainstream culture and fluent in English, ethnic minority children will avoid cultural biases on tests—as well as negative biases in the broader society.[31] Their performance will improve because they think and act like, and fit in with, people in the mainstream of their society.

Similarly, assimilation will enable ethnic minorities and the poor to more fully contribute to, and engage in, political processes. By becoming part of the cultural and linguistic mainstream, minorities will find it more possible to become active

---

[30] See the discussion in Boin et al. (2021).

[31] Research suggests that minorities also feel excluded from informal science and education centers, such as museums (see Dawson, 2014).

participants in politics. In this way, assimilation strengthens democracy, particularly by helping poor people of all ethnic groups (including poor Whites) to recognize their social class membership and collective interests.[32] The outcome will be a society where even poor citizens are able to participate in political actions on the basis of their own group interests, rather than act in ways that only serve the interests of the rich.

Benefits of Group Cohesion and Common Identity

During my visits to Japan, I have been struck by one of the claims that get repeated by some Japanese people when they try to explain the successes of Japanese society: historically, uniformity in the people of Japan has helped the nation remain cohesive and perform at a high level. The idea that more uniform groups are more cohesive and perform better receives research support.[33] In discussions about group cohesion of societies such as Japan, a closely related topic that often arises is that of a shared identity. The proposal is that in a society where people are more assimilated, they come to identify with one another and to see everyone as belonging to the same common group. Psychological research endorses the benefits of a shared common group.[34]

The focus in assimilation policy is the transformation of individuals to become more similar to one another. This takes place either through the transformation of minority group members to become more like the majority group (minority assimilation) or the transformation of both minority and majority group members to "melt into" one another and create a new identity (melting-pot assimilation). Irrespective of which path to assimilation is followed, supporters of assimilation argue that it results in a more cohesive society with a common identity.

Also, assimilation policy tends to be associated with stronger nationalism, and a stronger national identity. The nature of this national identity will vary, depending on whether the actual policy followed is closer to minority assimilation or melting-pot assimilation. Minority assimilation will lead to a national identity centered on the identity of the majority group. This identity is historically well-established, dominated by the culture of the majority group. In contrast, melting-pot assimilation leads to a new national identity, shaped by the fusion of different minority and majority group cultures. Many different groups contribute to this new national identity. At least this is one interpretation of the new American identity and culture that emerged from the coming together of so many different groups of people in the "promised land."[35] Out of the merging of so many different people from around the

---

[32] The issue of poverty and the challenges faced by the poor are discussed in Moghaddam (2023b).

[33] Beal et al. (2003); Mullen and Cooper (1994).

[34] Gaertner and Dovidio (2000). In addition to psychological research, research on immigration shows that more universalist individuals are more accepting of immigrants (Davidov et al., 2020).

[35] Moghaddam (2008, p. 131).

world, there evolved the new American culture, as well as the new "Americans"—unique in their identity and outlook.

Concluding Comment

Assimilation policy has the advantage of being in line with globalization. Supporters of assimilation argue that the economic, technological, and other forces fueling globalization are also forcing assimilation to take place at the global level. Societies, communities, and individuals are being pushed by globalization forces to become more similar to one another, and this has important advantages. Irrespective of whether the new emergent cohesiveness and collective identity arises through the influence of both minority and majority groups, or mainly or only through majority group influence, the results are greater cohesiveness and a stronger sense of common identity. Societies that are more cohesive and share a common identity are also better able to achieve their common goals and make progress.

References

Allport, G. W. (1954). *The nature of prejudice*. Addison-Wesley.

Baldwin, J. (1997). If Black English isn't a language, then tell me what is? *The Black Scholar: Journal of Black Studies and Research, 27*, 5–6.

Beal, D. J., Cohen, R. B., Burke, M. J., & McLendon, C. L. (2003). Cohesion and performance in groups: A meta-analytic clarification of construct relations. *Journal of Applied Psychology, 88*, 989–1004.

Berscheid, E., & Reis, H. T. (1998). Attraction and close relationships. In D. T. Gilbert, S. T. Fiske, & G. Lindzey (Eds.), *The handbook of social psychology* (Vol. 2, 4th ed., pp. 193–281). McGraw Hill.

Boin, J., Rupar, M., Graf, S., Neji, S., Spiegler, O., & Swart, H. (2021). The generalization of intergroup contact effects: Emerging research, policy relevance, and future directions. *Journal of Social Issues, 77*, 105–131.

Borden, R. S. (2014). The English only movement: Revisiting cultural hegemony. *Multicultural Perspectives, 16*, 229–233.

Byrne, D. (1971). *The attraction paradigm*. Academic Press.

Carreira, M., & Kagan, O. (2011). The results of the National Heritage Language Survey: Implications for teaching, curriculum design, and professional development. *Foreign Language Annals, 44*, 40–64.

Davidov, E., Seddig, D., Gorodzeisky, A., Raijman, R., Schmidt, P., & Semyonov, M. (2020). Direct and indirect predictors of opposition to immigration in Europe: Individual values, cultural values, and symbolic threat. *Journal of Ethnic and Migration Studies, 46*, 553–573.

Dawson, E. (2014). "Not designed for us": How science museums and science centers socially exclude low-income, minority ethnic groups. *Science Education, 98*, 981–1008.

Dinesen, P. T., Schaeffer, M., & Sønderskov, K. M. (2020). Ethnic diversity and social trust: A narrative and meta-analytic review. *Annual Review of Political Science, 23*, 441–465.

Dovidio, J. F., Gaertner, S. L., & Kawakami, K. (2003). Intergroup contact: The past, present, and the future. *Group Processes & Intergroup Relations, 6*, 5–21.

Ezedike, E. U. (2019). Multi-culturalism in education: A critical assessment of the impact of colonization and globalization on indigenous African values. *AFRREV IJAH: An International Journal of Arts and Humanities., 8,* 11 17.

Foddy, M., Platow, M. J., & Yamagishi, T. (2009). Group-based trust in strangers: The role of stereotypes and expectations. *Psychological Science, 20,* 419–422.

Gaertner, S. L., & Dovidio, J. F. (2000). *Reducing intergroup bias: The common group identity model.* Psychology Press.

Garcés-Mascareñas, B., & Penninx, R. (Eds.). (2016). *Integration processes and policies in Europe: Contexts, levels, and actors.* Springer Open.

Kobrin, S. J. (2020). How globalization became a thing that goes bump in the night. *Journal of International Business Policy, 3,* 280–286.

Kurt, I. (2023). World citizenship and the role of education in transition to global situations: One world one homeland. *Journal of Research in Social Sciences and Language, 3,* 70–80.

Hewstone, M., & Brown, R. J. (1986). Contact is not enough: An intergroup perspective on the contact hypothesis. In M. Hewstone & R. J. Brown (Eds.), *Contact and conflict in intergroup encounters* (pp. 3–44). Blackwell.

Hinton, L. (1999). Trading tongues: Loss of heritage languages in the United States. *English Today, 15,* 21–30.

Melchers, G., Shaw, P., & Sundkvist, P. (2019). *World Englishes* (3rd ed.). Taylor & Francis.

Moghaddam, F. M. (1998). *Social psychology: Exploring universals in social behavior.* Freeman.

Moghaddam, F. M. (2008). *Multiculturalism and intergroup relations: Implications for democracy in global context.* American Psychological Association Press.

Moghaddam, F. M. (2023a). *Political plasticity: The future of democracy and dictatorship.* Cambridge University Press.

Moghaddam, F. M. (2023b). *How psychologists failed: We neglected the poor and minorities, favored the rich and privileged, and got science wrong.* Cambridge University Press.

Montoya, R. M., Horton, R. S., & Kirchner, J. (2008). Is actual similarity necessary for attraction? A meta-analysis of actual and perceived similarity. *Journal of Social and Personal Relationships, 25,* 889–922.

Montoya, R. M., & Horton, R. S. (2012). A meta-analytic investigation of the processes underlying the similarity-attraction effect. *Journal of Social and Personality Relationships, 30,* 64–94.

Mullen, B., & Cooper, C. (1994). The relation between group cohesiveness and performance: An integration. *Psychological Bulletin, 115,* 210–227.

Osbeck, L., Moghaddam, F. M., & Perreault, S. (1997). Similarity and attraction among majority and minority groups in a multicultural context. *International Journal of Intercultural Relations, 21,* 113–123.

Park, R. E. (1950). *Race and culture.* Free Press.

Park, R. E., & Burgess, E. W. (1921). *Introduction to the science of society.* University of Chicago Press.

Pettigrew, T. F. (2021). Advancing intergroup contact theory: Comments on the issue's articles. *Journal of Social Issues, 77,* 258–273.

Pettigrew, T. F., & Tropp, L. R. (2006). A meta-analytic test of intergroup contact theory. *Journal of Personality and Social Psychology, 90,* 751–783.

Portes, A., & Manning, R. D. (2019). The immigrant enclave: Theory and empirical examples. In D. B. Grusky (Ed.), *Social stratification: Class, race, and gender in sociological perspective* (2nd ed., pp. 568–579). Routledge.

Salas-Schweikart et al., (under review).

Tan, J. H. W., & Vogel, C. (2008). Religion and trust: An experimental study. *Journal of Economic Psychology, 29,* 832–848.

Turner, F. J. (1920). *The frontier in American life.* Holt.

Zangwill, I. (1909). *The melting pot: Drama in four acts.* Macmillan.

Zou, L. X., & Cheryan, S. (2017). Two axes of subordination: A new model of racial position. *Journal of Personality and Social Psychology, 112,* 696–717.

Chapter 4
Rethinking Assimilation

In the ideal, then, assimilation is in line with meritocracy, and leads to societies that are more homogeneous and unified by a common collective identity. Because assimilation involves both minority group and majority group members acquiring the same basic linguistic and cultural characteristics, all individuals will be (in theory, at least) similarly equipped to compete on a level playing field in education, in employment, in politics, and in the wider economic marketplace. Also, because assimilation policy will lead to more homogeneous societies with shared common identities, these societies will be more cohesive and peaceful, so it is argued by supporters of assimilation (and integration). Intergroup discrimination and conflict will be minimized.

However, in practice assimilation policy is confronted by a number of challenges, partly because certain human behaviors have proven to be low in political plasticity, and highly resilient and difficult to change. For example, one such pattern is reflected in how we humans distribute ourselves spatially. Travel around any large city in many parts of the world, walk into a school cafeteria at lunchtime or a school playground when the children have a break from class, and you will notice a clear pattern. Individuals are not randomly distributed across the city, and they are not randomly distributed in the school cafeteria or playground—their distribution follows a pattern, with ethnic similarity being a strong factor shaping how people are distributed spatially and who they interact with.

Across large cities, ethnicity is a major factor that shapes housing patterns. In school cafeterias and playgrounds, ethnicity has a powerful influence on which particular children sit next to one another in the cafeteria and play with one another in the playground. This is as true in Western European countries as it is in the traditional immigrant-receiving countries of North America, Australia, and New Zealand. And it is as true in a strongly assimilationist country such as France as it is in multicultural countries such as Canada. Just as children form clusters based on ethnicity in "assimilationist" France, they form such clusters in "multicultural" Canada. This resilient and widespread pattern poses a problem for assimilation policy.

Below I discuss a number of such limitations to assimilation policy and point out how this policy leads to dead ends.

Contact and Assimilation

At a foundational level, assimilation policy assumes the validity of the contact hypothesis, proposing that contact between groups will reduce intergroup prejudice, discrimination, and conflict. As discussed in Chap. 3 of this text, Gordon Allport and other pioneering researchers concluded that contact will only improve intergroup relations under certain conditions. I proposed in Chap. 3 that these conditions are in practice very difficult to achieve. However, in the twenty-first century, researchers have arrived at far more optimistic conclusions, to the effect that contact leads to positive outcomes *irrespective* of the conditions set out by Gordon Allport. This is a dramatic turnaround. Are these new, optimistic conclusions convincing? The answer is no, not when we consider intergroup interactions in everyday life. In the world outside research studies, the salience of Allport's conditions for the positive outcomes of intergroup contact become more compelling.

In practice, it is clear that Allport was correct: contact only leads to improved intergroup relations under certain conditions (i.e., the two groups should enjoy equal status, be in a cooperative relationship, share common goals, and have intergroup contact in the context of a supportive community). When these conditions are not met, then increased contact will not result in better intergroup relations. For example, imagine a home occupied by slave owners, where slaves carry out the cleaning, cooking, childcare, and other everyday tasks both inside and outside the house. There will be a great deal of contact between slave owners and slaves in this house, but it does not lead to improved intergroup relations. The female slaves typically look after young children, some young female slaves might be forced to sleep with the White master of the house (their owner), and some child slaves might spend time amusing and playing games with their master's children. However, the context of these relationships is the institution of slavery, and increased contact between slave owners and slaves does not improve intergroup relations.

Fay Yarbrough reports distressing but revealing narratives of former slaves in the southern parts of the United States, relating how slave owners could have very close contact with some female slaves and have children with them. Despite the very close contact between slave masters and their slave mistresses, Yarbrough reports that slave owners would regularly sell the women they slept with, and they would even "…sell their own children by slave women just like he would any others."[1] Clearly, the conditions of contact between slave owners and slaves meant that no

---

[1] Yarbrough (2005, pp. 570–571).

matter how close, intimate, and regular the contact was, it would not improve the relationship between the two groups.

It might be argued that the era of slavery is over, and a more optimistic view of intergroup contact is more applicable to the twenty-first century. Unfortunately, this argument is not convincing in either Western or non-Western societies. Let us first consider an example from outside the Western context. In countries such as Afghanistan and Iran, in the twenty-first century, women are being treated as third-class citizens. In both countries, women have *lost* basic rights in recent years. An obvious example is when women appear in public. If women fail to conform to draconian *hijab* rules, they are severely punished—through the orders of male judges (women are forbidden to be judges in Afghanistan and Iran, because they are considered too emotional and mentally incapable of making rational judgements!). According to the logic of the optimistic research on intergroup contact, the barbaric treatment of women in Afghanistan and Iran is because there is too little contact between males and females in these societies. The idea that more contact will lead to improved male-female relations in Afghanistan and Iran is obviously nonsensical.

But what about intergroup contact irrespective of conditions leading to improved intergroup relations in Western contexts? Consider the situation of upper-middle class families in the United States, and their relationship with Hispanic workers who look after children, clean houses, do the gardening, and clean swimming pools and cars, along with a long list of other tasks. In many cases, these Hispanic workers interact with their upper-middle class employers on an everyday basis, sometimes living in the same house (e.g., in the case of Hispanic nannies). But does this kind of continuous contact improve intergroup relations? We could add additional examples—such as relations between company owners and employees, managers, and workers—all illustrative of the importance of the *conditions* stipulated by Allport, and leading to the same conclusion that contact only leads to improved intergroup relations under certain conditions.

Becoming Similar and the Need for Distinctiveness

The goal of assimilation policy is to engage both minority and majority group members in a process of gradual transformation, with individuals becoming increasingly more similar to one another and adopting a common, shared identity. Allegiance to, and affiliation with, nations, language groups, ethnic groups, and other groups of origin will gradually decline, as identification with the adopted host nation becomes stronger. A proposed advantage of this approach, as discussed in Chap. 3 of this text, is that society benefits from the robust relationship between similarity and attraction. The idea is that as minority and majority groups become more similar, people get to like and trust one another. But this rosy picture of a homogeneous nation, unified under one shared identity, leaves out a vitally important characteristic of human behavior: the universal need for standing apart and being different.

The need to be different, to stand out as distinct, probably arose through evolutionary processes, already touched in Chap. 1 of this text in discussions of the "in search of group differences movement." In competition with one another, humans developed the strategy of discovering vacant spaces, where new resources could be accessed. For example, if people found that there were too many hunters targeting the same group of animals at the same time in the same geographical area, they would (among other changes) move to new areas with sparser or no human populations and in this way gain access to more food with less competition. This drive to find vacant spaces and to differentiate also extends to human identities.

The need for a distinct identity is central to social identity theory, a highly influential theory developed by Henri Tajfel (1919–1982), John Turner (1947–2011), and other European social psychologists from the 1970s.[2] Social identity theory proposes that humans are motivated to achieve an identity that is *both* positive and distinct. An intriguing development from the theory, backed by empirical evidence, is the idea that under certain conditions, similarity can result in a feeling of threat.[3] For example, imagine you support a particular sports team (I support Tottenham Hotspur soccer club), and another soccer fan praises your team, but adds that although your team is very good, it is exactly the same as another team in the league. "In fact, I really can't tell the difference between your team and that other team," the soccer fan adds. According to social identity theory, this positioning of your team as the same as another team is threatening to you, because although your team is described as being "very good," it is not depicted as having a distinct identity.

A shortcoming of assimilation policy is that although the need for achieving a positive identity is satisfied, the need for achieving a distinct identity is not. This becomes an even more serious problem in minority assimilation, where minorities are expected to take on the characteristics of the majority group. But often minority group members feel that they can never become exactly the same as majority group members; at best, they can only become "good copies."[4] In these situations, minorities lose their distinctiveness, but can never become the same as majority group members.

Greater Similarities within Nations, but Greater Differences between Nations

As things stand, assimilation is being put into practice in ways that lead to greater homogeneity within societies. For example, government funding and control of public education systems are being used to teach children the mainstream language.

---

[2] For the original theory, see Tajfel and Turner (1979); for a broader discussion of social identity theory in the context of other intergroup theories, see Moghaddam (2008).

[3] Moghaddam and Stringer (1988); Mummendey and Schreiber (1983).

[4] The good copy problem was first discussed in Moghaddam (2006, pp. 36–38).

Through language, children take on a core common culture and national identity, which distinguishes between "their nation" and other nations. By way of everyday interactions and affiliations, such as with national sports teams competing in the Olympics and other international competitions, each new generation learns to think and act as a nationalist. The differences between their nation and other nations become further exaggerated and celebrated. National identity seeps into the banal activities of everyday life, so that even the most mundane behaviors endorse nationalism and national differences.[5]

Particularly since the 1960s, there has been a politization of nationalism. Left-wing critics have depicted nationalism as dangerous, a means by which authoritarian leaders can mobilize support through blind allegiance to "the nation." It has been argued that authoritarian leaders such as Donald Trump can mobilize popular support simply by wrapping themselves in the American flag and proclaiming "America First." More enlightened mass education has been proposed as a solution to this kind of blind nationalism. But the solution may not be easy to achieve, because of the strong emotions tied up with nationalism. Andreas Wimmer has argued that "Nationalism is not an irrational sentiment that can be banished from contemporary politics through enlightening education…".[6]

While assimilation within societies strengthens nationalism, this kind of assimilation does not work with or highlight the common characteristics of *all* humans. Rather, the focus in assimilation within societies is on the characteristics of the majority group that the minority groups should take on (minority-assimilation) or the characteristics that emerge from the melting together of all groups (melting-pot assimilation) in each particular society. As a result, the shared characteristics of people that emerge through assimilation policy within nations are only what is shared as common characteristics within each particular society. The outcome is that differences between nations continue to be highlighted and can actually increase, so that nations are seen as more different from one another. Thus, assimilation functioning at the national level can result in many different nations each having internal cohesion and each being united in a common national identity, but the differences and gaps between these nations could be enormous and even increasing—fertile ground for internation conflicts.

Increasingly Unequal Outcomes and the Myth of Meritocracy

One of the complaints I routinely hear about the current system of selecting students for competitive universities is that the tests being used are culturally biased against minorities. It is argued that these selection tests favor students who represent the majority culture. This criticism seems to provide further support for assimilation

---

[5] Billig (1995).
[6] Wimmer (2019, p. 28).

(and integration) policy. In a situation where all students have assimilated into the same culture and language, then if there is bias in university selection tests, all students will be affected in the same way (presumably, they will all benefit). The selection system will be more meritocratic. However, a counterargument is that entrance to competitive universities is most significantly influenced by family wealth, and increasing wealth inequality is *not* addressed by assimilation policy.[7]

First, evidence demonstrates that wealth inequality is increasing across most parts of the world, including in countries as varied as the United States, the United Kingdom, and China.[8] According to Oxfam, "Billionaire fortunes are increasing by $2.7 billion a day even as at least 1.7 billion workers are now living in countries where inflation is outpacing wages."[9] Second, the cost of university education is sharply increasing, so that even middle-class families are forced to make huge sacrifices when they send their children for further education.[10] Children from lower-class families face enormous financial challenges when they attempt to pursue university education. Financial factors are the most important reason why students from rich families are enormously overrepresented at the more competitive universities.[11]

Thus, the claim that assimilation (integration) policy leads to a more level playing field and supports meritocracy is highly questionable. At present the playing field is extremely uneven and assimilation will not make it fairer. For example, the more competitive the university, the greater the percentage of its students who are from rich families. The selection tests used for university admissions work in favor of the rich.[12]

Democracy, Peace, and Assimilation

Probably the strongest argument in favor of assimilation policy is that it leads to a more peaceful, democratic society. The goal of assimilation is for everyone to develop similar cultural and linguistic characteristics, resulting in a more homogeneous society. As a consequence, it can be argued, there will not be group differences—at least, not important ones—that could serve as the basis of intergroup rifts and conflicts. Society will be more peaceful. Also, it is argued that cultural and linguistic similarity will enable everyone to participate more equally in the democratic process. Minorities will be better represented and this will result in a healthier

---

[7] For a discussion of the research literature on wealth and performance in education, see Moghaddam (2023, ch.3).

[8] Atkinson (2015), Piketty (2014), The Economist (2021, June 26, p. 12).

[9] Oxfam (2023).

[10] Zaloom (2019).

[11] Carnevale and Strohl (2013).

[12] Sternberg (2015).

democracy. But upon deeper probing, underlying this rosy picture of the benefits of assimilation (integration) policy are a number of assumptions that prove to be questionable.

First, it is assumed that in order for intergroup bias and conflict to arise, there need to be objectively important differences between groups. When we consider major conflicts within societies, at first glance these conflicts seem to arise because of enormously important intergroup differences. Consider, for example, the conflict between the Hutu and the Tutsi in Rwanda, which resulted in about a million people being slaughtered in 1994.[13] There are many other contemporary examples, particularly concerning religious groups, such as Catholics and Protestants in Ireland, and Sunni and Shi'a Muslims in Iraq. In each of these cases, violent conflicts have resulted in thousands of deaths. The assumption is that underlying these bloody conflicts, there must be objectively important differences between the groups engaged in the fighting.

But both experimental evidence and everyday experiences show that intergroup biases and conflicts can arise even when differences between groups are objectively unimportant; indeed, intergroup differences can be objectively trivial and still lead to violent intergroup conflict. The key determinant is not the objective importance of intergroup differences but the subjective interpretation and social construction of intergroup differences. Even objectively trivial differences between groups can be used as an excuse to be biased against, and inflict violence upon, an outgroup.

First, experimental evidence from the minimal group paradigm demonstrates the power of objectively trivial differences in intergroup bias.[14] The goal of the minimal group paradigm experiments is to create groups that are as meaningless as possible, and then test for intergroup bias. In a typical experiment, participants first carry out a trivial task, such as estimating the number of dots on a screen. Participants are then placed in group "X" or group "Y" (ostensibly) on the basis of how they responded on the dot-estimation task. In the second part of the study, participants allocate points to the members of group "X" and group "Y." Participants do not receive any of the points they allocate, they do not know the identities of group "Y" or group "X" members, they do not expect to interact with any members of group "Y" or group "X," and there is no value assigned by the experimenter to the points being allocated. Despite the objectively trivial basis of differences between groups "Y" and "X" and the lack of objective reasons to show bias, there is a tendency for participants (at least in Western societies) to allocate more points to their own groups.

It is not the objective importance of the differences between groups that shapes the behavior of participants in the minimal group paradigm but the meaning(s) participants choose to give to intergroup differences. This interpretation is supported by research that shows the influence of an objectively trivial and an objectively important intergroup difference to be the same, when in an experimental context the

---

[13] Uvin (1997).

[14] For the original minimal group paradigm studies, see Tajfel (1970). For a broader discussion of these experiments, see Moghaddam (2008, ch. 5).

groups are different from one another in only one way (either objectively trivial or objectively important difference between the two groups).[15] The social construction of meaning is also evident in how groups attend to, or even manufacture and fabricate, differences between ingroups and outgroups in everyday life.

Sport is an example of human activity that routinely involves the manufacture of, and giving importance to, intergroup differences. Consider two soccer teams playing in a cup final. The teams wear different colors and have different names. Each team tries to kick the ball into the opponent's goal. An alien visitor to planet earth might see this as an unimportant activity. After all, it involves 22 players chasing and kicking a ball for 90 minutes. But this "unimportant" activity is interpreted as extremely important by millions of fans, and sometimes billions of people watch on television. Such soccer matches are extremely important because people *ascribe them* importance.

Similarly, differences between Sunni and Shi'a Muslims, Catholics and Protestants, and other religious groups might not be objectively that important, but they can be interpreted as important by believers. I spent my first 8 years of life in Tehran, Iran, where I played with other children in my neighborhoods, some of them from families that were Sunni Muslim (I was born Shi'a Muslim), Armenian, Zoroastrian, and other non-Shi'a Muslim faiths. At that time in Iran, far less attention was given to religious affiliation. After the 1979 revolution and the coming to power of fanatical mullahs in Iran, the atmosphere has changed, and religious affiliation is given the highest importance because of the values endorsed by the Iranian dictatorship.

The importance given to religious affiliation has also varied across time in Ireland, where the population is mostly Catholic and Protestant. At times in Irish history, the relationship between these two groups has been relatively peaceful, but at other times it has been ferociously antagonistic and bloody. But when I visited Ireland in the mid-1970s, during a period of particularly intense Catholic-Protestant violence, I was very surprised at how similar I found the two groups to be. While Catholics and Protestants in Ireland at that time were focused on their differences, as an outsider I was struck by how much they have in common. Their differences could be interpreted as relatively minor—but this is another example of how small differences can be ascribed significance and interpreted as highly important.

An implication is that no matter how objectively similar people become through assimilation (integration) policy, there will always be available some differences between groups that could be highlighted, given significance, and used as a basis for intergroup bias and conflict. Even if differences between groups do not exist, they can be manufactured. For example, as the time of the Rwandan genocide stereotypes of the Tutsi and the Hutu were largely fabricated to present an image of there being huge differences between them. Despite the fabricated nature of differences between the Tutsi and the Hutu, people murdered outgroup members in very large numbers.

---

[15] Moghaddam and Stringer (1986).

Concluding Comment

Assimilation (integration) policy has merits (as discussed in Chap. 3), but we have reviewed in this chapter how it also has a number of fatal shortcomings. Influencing people to become more and more similar neglects the need people have for distinctiveness. Nor does giving priority to similarity solve the problem of growing wealth inequalities, which is at the basis of unequal outcomes in education, work, and other domains. The same growing wealth inequalities also impact the influence people have in political processes and outcomes.

Most importantly, bias, discrimination, and conflict between groups are not always on the basis of objectively important intergroup differences. Groups can and do manufacture differences between themselves and outgroups, and they often give importance to intergroup differences that are objectively trivial. Consequently, a society in which individuals are objectively more and more similar can still be riddled with intergroup discrimination and conflict, because groups can act on the basis of what are objectively "trivial" differences between them.

It is imperative that certain adaptations are made to assimilation policy. First, it is not enough that people assimilate to become similar according to a particular national identity—there has to be some room for between-group differences. Second, the basis of similarity needs to be more than national identity through either minority assimilation or melting-pot assimilation. A focus on, and priority given to, existing and continuous human commonalities is far more promising. All human beings have a great deal in common, and this is a substantial basis for joint action to safeguard our future in the face of global warming and other challenges.

References

Atkinson, A. (2015). *Inequality: What can be done?* Harvard University Press.

Billig, M. (1995). *Banal nationalism.* Sage.

Carnevale, A. P., & Strohl, J. (2013). *Separate & unequal: How higher education reinforces the intergenerational reproduction of White racial privilege.* Georgetown Public Policy Institute. https://cew.georgetown.edu/cew-reports/separate-unequal/

Moghaddam, F. M. (2006). *From the terrorists' point of view: What they experience and why they come to destroy.* Praeger Security International Series.

Moghaddam, F. M. (2008). *Multiculturalism and intergroup relations: Implications for democracy in global context.* American Psychological Association Press.

Moghaddam, F. M. (2023). *How psychologists failed: We neglected the poor and minorities, favored the rich and privileged, and got science wrong.* Cambridge University Press.

Moghaddam, F. M., & Stringer, P. (1986). "Important" and "trivial" criteria in the minimal group paradigm. *Journal of Social Psychology, 126*, 345–354.

Moghaddam, F. M., & Stringer, P. (1988). Outgroup similarity and intergroup bias. *Journal of Social Psychology, 128*, 105–115.

Mummendey, A., & Schreiber, H. J. (1983). Better or just different? Positive social identity by discrimination against, or by differentiation from, outgroups. *European Journal of Social Psychology, 13*, 301–313.

Oxfam. (2023). *Richest 1% bag nearly twice as much wealth as the rest of the world put together over the past two years*. https://www.oxfam.org/en/press-releases/richest-1-bag-nearly-twice-much-wealth-rest world put together over past two years#:~:text=The%20richest%201%20 percent%20grabbed,half%20of%20all%20new%20wealth. Accessed Aug 5, 2023.

Piketty, T. (2014). *Capital in the twenty-first century* (Trans. A. Goldhammer). The Belknap Press of Harvard University Press.

Sternberg, R. J. (2015). Successful intelligence: A model for testing intelligence beyond IQ tests. *European Journal of Education and Psychology, 8*, 76–84.

Tajfel, H. (1970). Experiments in intergroup discrimination. *Scientific American, 223*, 96–108.

Tajfel, H., & Turner, J. C. (1979). An integrative theory of intergroup conflict. In W. G. Austin & S. Worchel (Eds.), *The social psychology of intergroup relations* (pp. 33–47). Brooks/Cole.

The Economist. (2021). *Special report: The Chinese Communist Party*. June 26, pp. 1–12.

Wimmer, A. (2019). Why nationalism works. *Foreign Affairs, 98*, 27–34.

Uvin, P. (1997). Prejudice, crisis, and genocide in Rwanda. *African Studies Review, 40*, 91–115.

Yarbrough, F. A. (2005). Power, perception, and interracial sex: Former slaves recall a multiracial South. *The Journal of Southern History, 71*, 599–588.

Zaloom, C. (2019). *Indebted: How families make college work at any cost*. Princeton University Press.

Chapter 5
Presenting Multiculturalism

Multiculturalism is among the most influential cultural and political movements to sweep across the world since the Second World War (1939–1945).[1] Although some leading politicians have claimed that multiculturalism has failed, objective assessments of trends in 21 Western democracies reveal that "…despite the perception of a backlash and retreat from immigrant multiculturalism…multiculturalism policies have persisted, and in many cases, continue to expand."[2] At the simplest descriptive level, any society that is ethnoculturally diverse is "multicultural."[3] However, as discussed below, multiculturalism also has other requirements.[4] In terms of how multiculturalism is achieved, I have made a broad distinction between laissez-faire *multiculturalism*, where market forces determine the diversity mix in society, and *planned multiculturalism*, where the government directly intervenes to influence diversity levels.[5] For example, such intervention can be through policies to promote or restrict immigration from particular parts of the world, and/or to support heritage culture retention among minority groups. In this discussion, the main focus is on planned multiculturalism, as first put into practice by the governments of Canada (1972) and Australia (1978).

---

[1] The literature on multiculturalism is extensive (Moghaddam, 2008), and in recent years the critical discussions around multiculturalism have also expanded (Berry, 2023; Shorten, 2022). In the Canadian context, Berry et al. (1977) distinguished between three aspects of multiculturalism: diversity as it exists in Canadian society, the desire of Canadians to maintain and share diversity, and government policy toward diversity.

[2] See the Multiculturalism Policy Index, https://www.queensu.ca/mcp/about.

[3] Following Berry et al. (1977).

[4] This ideal is not realized, as reflected in critical discussions of "revolutionary multiculturalism," intended to actually push societies toward the multicultural ideal (McLaren, 2018).

[5] Moghaddam (2008, ch. 8).

F. M. Moghaddam, *The Psychology of Multiculturalism, Assimilation, and Omniculturalism*, SpringerBriefs in Psychology, https://doi.org/10.1007/978-3-031-62597-8_5

The point of departure for multiculturalism is toleration of diversity. Of course, there have been regimes of toleration in the past, such as the five examples that Michael Walzer identifies in history.[6] But contemporary multiculturalism goes beyond Walzer's historical regimes of toleration.

Contemporary Multiculturalism

A number of propositions underlie contemporary multiculturalism. Some of these propositions are explicit, but others remain implicit. The starting proposition is that people have the right to live in societies where all are supported on equal terms to retain their ethnocultural and other heritage group characteristics, including the heritage language. Second, ethnocultural groups are recognized by others as having equal worth relative to other groups. Third, group members are open to sharing their group cultures with outgroup members. Fourth, intergroup differences are recognized and celebrated. Fifth, their confidence in their own identities and cultures leads them to be open and accepting toward outgroup members who have different group identities and cultures. There is a sixth component that underlies all the first five: the claim that the government should support multiculturalism in both the public and private sectors, including in education. These key components make contemporary multiculturalism different from the kinds of diversity tolerated in the past, such as during the time of the Roman Empire.

The twenty-first-century context also makes contemporary multiculturalism unique. There is no doubt that diversity did exist in earlier eras, such as in the British Empire during the nineteenth century, but contemporary globalization is associated with a high level of global population movement at unprecedentedly rapid speeds. Contemporary mass transportation means that millions of people now move rapidly out of war regions to seek shelter in other regions. For example, millions have moved quickly in the twenty-first century from the Middle East region and from Ukraine to find shelter in Europe and North America (resulting in sudden intergroup contact, as discussed in Chap. 2 of this text). As a consequence of mass transportation, then, the level of diversity in a society can very quickly increase, or decrease.

Unfortunately, in some parts of the world, prejudice, discrimination, and outright aggression toward minorities have resulted in decreased diversity, such as in parts of the Near and Middle East.[7] This trend has particularly impacted religious minorities, who have become targets with the rise of radical Islam, as reflected in the treatment of the Yazidi minority in Iraq at the hands of the Islamic State terrorist group in the mid-2010s. Under pressure from radical Islam, the number of Christians in a number of countries in the Near and Middle East has declined (religious minorities

---

[6] Walzer (1997).

[7] Longva and Roald (2012).

are also under pressure from groups of extremist Jews in Israel).[8] Armenians, Jews, and other religious minorities have also left Iran and some other parts of the Near and Middle East, because of government policies enforcing radical Islam and pressuring minorities. In 2023 over 100,000 Armenians were forced to flee the Nagorno-Karabakh region, resulting in Azerbaijan becoming more uniformly Muslim. Thus, although it is true that immigration is leading most Western societies to become more diverse in the twenty-first century, as Robert Putnam and others have claimed, it is also important to point out that the persecution of religious minorities is resulting in decreased diversity in some other societies, such as in the Near and Middle East.[9] The result is two contrasting trends: at the same time as there is declining diversity in some societies, there is increased diversity in many others.

Another characteristic of contemporary multiculturalism that is new is the avowed goal of reaching particular types and levels of diversity. The Roman Empire 2000 years ago and the British Empire in the nineteenth century both included diverse populations, but there was no explicit value assigned—as there is today—to having this diversity be reflected in the makeup of government organizations, institutions (e.g., schools and other training centers), or important decision-making groups. Achieving a certain level of diversity is now seen to be beneficial at work, in schools, among academic and medical professionals, in military leadership, and in leadership broadly in both private and government sectors.[10] Diversity is interpreted as a positive characteristic of a business organization, government decision-making body, and academic institution.[11] Correspondingly, lack of diversity is seen as a shortcoming and a weakness. Optimal performance is associated with higher diversity.[12] This is a new perspective on the composition of human groups.

Below I further discuss the six main desired characteristics of contemporary multiculturalism.

People Are Supported Equally to Retain Their Heritage Group Characteristics

…my discovering my own identity doesn't mean that I work it out in isolation, but that I negotiate it through dialogue, partly overt, partly internal, with others…My own identity crucially depends on my dialogical relations with others. Charles Taylor.[13]

A point of departure for contemporary multiculturalism is the proposition that, first, identity is of great importance and, second, that identity evolves through a

---

[8] Womack (2020).

[9] Putnam (2007).

[10] For example, diversity improves performance in healthcare (Gomez & Bernet, 2019).

[11] For example, see discussions of diversity benefits in education (Goethe & Colina, 2018).

[12] For example, problem-solving by diverse groups is more effective (Hong & Page, 2004).

[13] Taylor (1992, p. 34).

dialogical process, whereby others play an essential role in shaping one's sense of identity.

The importance of group identity has been highlighted by both academic researchers and the practical experiences of minority and majority groups. In terms of academic research, since the 1970s, a movement led by European researchers has illuminated the importance of social identity, defined by Henri Tajfel (1919–1982) as "...that part of an individual's self-concept which derives from his knowledge of his membership in a social group (or groups) together with the value and emotional significance attached to that membership."[14] Social identity, as well as the self broadly, emerges through socialization processes, which begins in the earliest days of life.

It is through participation in collective life and interactions with others that a sense of self emerges. This perspective involves the conceptualization of development "from societies to cells' rather than the reductionist perspective of 'from cells to societies."[15] There are different theoretical perspectives on the development of the self and identity, but they all assume an important role for the social environment in how the self and identity take shape; others help to construct our conceptions of ourselves and the groups with which we identify.[16] The variety of terms used by different teams of researchers discussing the social processes of identity emergence— including "interactional" and "dialogical" processes of self-development—all assume that social context is central to identity development. The implication of the perspective that emerges from social and developmental research is that it is of the greatest importance how society supports groups, including gender and sexual orientation groups, as well as those defined in terms of ethnicity, culture, language, religion, and other heritage characteristics.

The first step taken by multiculturalism is the assertion that all heritage groups must be equally supported by the larger society. This equal support given to groups implies that children growing up in homes that are, for example, Christian, Jewish, Muslim, atheist, or any other faith tradition, and those growing up in families belonging to different ethnic and language groups, will all feel equally accepted in the larger society. The "equal support" provided to groups includes support from the justice system, according to which discrimination on the basis of gender, ethnicity, and such groupings is illegal.

The importance of group identity has also been demonstrated by the practical experiences of minority and majority groups: group identity is a key factor in the mobilization of people to take collective action, which is an essential part of democracy.[17] That is, people become part of a social movement and participate in collective action—from protesting online to protesting on the streets, from signing petitions to joining with their ingroup to oppose particular government policies,

---

[14] Tajfel (1978, p. 63).

[15] Moghaddam (2023).

[16] Mansfield (2000).

[17] Fominaya (2010); Polletta and Jasper (2001).

when they identify strongly enough with a particular group. For example, Tiana Gaudette and colleagues examined how right-wing extremists used the website *Reddit* (created in 2005) to post content, and attract like-minded others in communities referred to as *Subreddits*.[18] By giving an "upvote" to extremist right-wing content, like-minded right-wing extremists can mobilize their group, and develop their identity in opposition to liberals, traditional conservatives, and others they see as competitors and/or enemies.

But before the twenty-first-century surge of right-wing extremist movements, from the 1960s there were liberal-oriented collective movements among women, African Americans, gays, and other minorities. Participation in these collective movements was also influenced by strong identification with their ingroups.[19] This is in line with social identity theory predictions, which postulate that stronger identification with the ingroup will increase the probability of participation in collective action.[20] Not surprisingly, *Black Lives Matter* (BLM) and other similar minority movements have attempted to develop and adopt communications frames that increase identification with the ingroup (e.g., African Americans)—in the expectation that this will increase participation in collective action.[21] The desired outcome of such collective action is to influence the larger society to give equal recognition to all minority groups, and to give support to individual group members, so they are motivated to remain active in, and to ensure the survival of, their ingroups.

Thus, as a first step, multicultural societies provide equal support to the members of different groups to maintain their group memberships and group characteristics. Next, we discuss the evaluative component of the worth of each group.

Every Group Is Recognized as Having Equal Worth Relative to Other Groups

Research in the social identity tradition has shown that personal identity is in important respects dependent on social identity.[22] The kind of person we see ourselves to be depends in large part on the groups to which we feel we belong. Because we strive to achieve a positive and distinct personal identity, we are motivated to belong to groups that enjoy a positive and distinct identity (as discussed in Chap. 4 of this text).[23] It is not enough for a person to know that she belongs to a group that is positively evaluated; it is also important for her to know that her group is seen to be different from other groups in some important respect(s). But how does one come to

---

[18] Gaudette et al. (2021).

[19] Simon et al. (1998) demonstrate this with older people in Germany and gays in the United States.

[20] Thomas et al. (2020).

[21] Bonilla and Tillery (2020) provide examples of more successful frames.

[22] Tajfel (1978).

[23] Brown (2020) provides an insightful short assessment of the social identity approach.

know about the level of positiveness and distinctiveness of one's social identity? In the above discussion, we reviewed how personal and individual identity takes shape through dialogical processes involving social interactions with others, which result in the individual learning how others see her group. Integral to this social learning process are impressions of the extent to which others perceive one's ingroup as positive and distinct.

According to multiculturalism, heritage groups must not only receive equal support to continue to survive and effectively function, but they must also be treated as having equal worth. For example, in the context of the United States and Europe, ethnic minorities and White majority groups must feel that they are valued equally by the larger society. In the Canadian context, French-Canadians and English-Canadians must learn that they are of equal worth. Similarly, in non-Western societies with multiple languages and ethnicities (such as India and China), and in immigrant-receiving countries with indigenous peoples (such as Australia and New Zealand), the various groups must feel that they are equally valued by the larger society.

Given that there is enormous variation in the size, resources, histories, and other characteristics of different groups in a society, the goal of making all groups feel equally valued, so they all perceive that they have a positive and distinct identity, is a challenging one. However, governments can facilitate this process by providing a legal foundation to achieve a society in which groups are treated as having equal worth. At a minimum, the justice system (the formal laws of the land, law courts, and so on) must make group-based discrimination illegal. Beyond this, the members of different groups (e.g., different ethnic groups) must feel that their group is valued as equal to other groups.

The goal of achieving a society in which all important heritage groups feel equally valued includes "symbolic" domains such as clothing, as well as in cultural areas such as music and literature. For example, the assimilation policy practiced in France makes it illegal for children to wear religious symbols, including clothing such as the Islamic burqa and niqab, in public schools. This ban is a source of frustration and opposition for some traditional and fundamentalist Muslims, while some others who were born Muslim but became secular as adults support this ban.[24] But such a ban is not in line with multiculturalism, whereby the characteristics of different heritage groups are equally supported. Obviously, this reflects controversies and different paths adopted by multiculturalism and assimilation. In domains such as literature and music, also, there are controversies about assigning equal value to the products of all cultures. For example, do other cultures produce music of value equal to the music of Bach, Beethoven, and Mozart? Are some video games comparable to works of literature such as Ferdowsi's *Shahnameh*, Tolstoy's *War and Peace*, and Shakespeare's *Hamlet*? These questions lead us to discuss relativism and universal standards, in Chap. 6 of this text.

---

[24] Cohen-Almagor (2022) provides an insightful discussion of the debate on secularism and religious practices in France.

Group Members Are Open to Sharing Their Group Cultures with Outgroup Members

A proposition of multiculturalism that is central but has received less attention relative to other propositions is that group members should be open to sharing their cultures with people from other groups. This feature of multiculturalism is sometimes mentioned, but seldom critically discussed. I will focus on two aspects of this proposition. First, at the macro societal level, what is the function of this sharing of cultures across groups? The answer to this question further clarifies why this intergroup sharing is central to multiculturalism. Second, at the microlevel of individual and interpersonal processes, what factors are associated with the tendency of individuals to be open to sharing their cultures with outgroup members?

First, at the macro societal level, multiculturalism involves not just the retention of heritage group characteristics but also the sharing of one's own group cultures with outgroup members. People do not just stay within the confines of their own groups, but are actively open to other groups and sharing their own group characteristics and cultures with outgroups. In the ideal, this creates a dynamic society, in which there is a high level of communication, interaction, and cultural sharing between different groups.

The knowledge and understanding that people have of outgroups is intended to improve intergroup relations. Individuals learn about group distinctiveness: how outgroups are different from one another, as well as from ingroup(s), and how each group is in some ways distinct and different from all other groups. The foundation for celebrating group differences is formed in this way. Also, this understanding about group distinctiveness results in people appreciating the mosaic nature of multicultural societies, with citizens aware of how pieces of the mosaic fit within the whole.

At the microlevel, we need to consider how personality characteristics and interpersonal relations influence being open to sharing ingroup cultures and characteristics with outgroups. The most obvious personality trait to consider is "openness to experience," one of the so-called Big Five traits that are central to contemporary personality research.[25] Individuals who are higher on openness to experience tend to, among other things, have a preference for variety and be intellectually more curious and imaginative. Research confirms that individuals higher on openness to experience have more positive outgroup attitudes and more connections with outgroup members.[26] Openness to experience was also connected with more positive interracial interactions in societies characterized by diversity, such as the United States.[27]

But we should not limit our discussion to what I have termed *System M (Micro)* personality, which assumes intrapersonal factors to causally determine

---

[25] John (2021).

[26] Bobowik et al. (2022).

[27] Flynn (2005).

consistencies in behavior.[28] We should also consider what I have termed *System E (Extended)* personality, which assumes context and macro processes play a key role in shaping what is traditionally termed personality. System E personality points to life experiences as shaping behavior style. In line with this, research by David Sparkman and colleagues shows that individuals who are exposed to outgroup members and cultures report higher openness to experience and less outgroup prejudice.[29] The implication is that openness to experience and willingness to share cultures can be influenced by diversity management policies.

Intergroup Differences Are Celebrated

An aspect of multiculturalism that has made an enormous impact on everyday life, particularly in education, is the proposition that we should "celebrate our differences." The specific focus here is on differences between groups, such as groups that are different in terms of ethnicity, race, language, religion, and culture broadly. The idea is that in addition to recognizing and sharing group differences, we should highlight and celebrate them.

The idea of "celebrating our differences" has been particularly influential at all levels of education, from kindergarten to universities, and has become part of how topics such as grammar are taught to young children.[30] In educational television shows such as *Sesame Street*, young children are being taught that we should celebrate our differences (and the same message is communicated by Sesame Street books[31]). More broadly, popular books for children are also teaching that we should celebrate our differences. Examples are *Celebrating Our Differences: A coloring Book for Kids* by Francesco Hahn and *Celebrating Our Differences: Devi2Diva and the Power of Inclusivity* by Cathy Pearson.

The strength of the "celebrate our differences" movement is difficult to overstate. Step into any elementary school in North America, Europe, and many other parts of the world, and you are likely to see banners and posters declaring that we should celebrate our differences. The same trend is evident in the teaching of high school students and in online education; the celebration of differences is integral to multiculturalism, and multiculturalism has become central to contemporary school life for students, teachers, and administrators.[32]

The value system that lauds the celebration of differences between groups has had a number of important consequences for life in societies characterized by

---

[28] Moghaddam (2023, ch. 4).

[29] Sparkman et al. (2017).

[30] McCreight (2016).

[31] For example, see the Sesame Street book for young children *We're Different, We're the Same – and We're All Wonderful* by Bobbi Jane Kates.

[32] For example, see Woodley et al. (2017).

diversity. First, the high value given to intergroup differences means that people actively try to find such differences. During intergroup interactions, priority is given to differences between groups, with each individual asking "How are we different from one another?" Rather than, "How are we similar to one another?" An alternative to this multicultural approach is for people to look for similarities, and ask "How are we similar as human beings? What do we have in common as human beings?" Thus, the practice of celebrating differences means that within multicultural societies, people learn to identify, point to, and prioritize differences between groups.

But the high value placed on identifying and celebrating differences between groups can also lead, in some cases, to people constructing and fabricating differences between groups. That is, for example, people become creative in finding and manufacturing ways in which their group differs from, and enjoys positive characteristics, relative to other groups. The intergroup differences that are manufactured can be fictional, but still be related to already existing group stereotypes, and they could incorporate some elements of the imagined characteristics of the ingroup and outgroups. For example, when making comparisons between the ingroup and an outgroup that in their society is stereotyped as aggressive, ingroup members might refer to the "aggressive" stereotype of the outgroup and conclude that our group is peaceful and nonviolent, and we are very different from group "X," who are warmongers and hostile. This distinction between "we the peace-loving people" and "those hostile warmongers" could become part of the tradition of "celebrating differences," even though this intergroup difference may have no objective, factual basis. The value system of "celebrating differences" could lead to the celebration of group differences that were not recognized before, or in some cases did not even exist before. This is a topic we return to in Chap. 6 of this text.

Confidence in Ingroup Identities and Cultures Leads People to be Open and Accepting Toward Outgroup Members

What has been named the *multiculturalism hypothesis* asserts that feelings of confidence in one's own identity will lead one to be open and accepting toward outgroup members. This is in line with assumptions underlying the "self-esteem movement," arguing that many behavioral problems arise because of damaged, low self-esteem.[33] By improving the self-esteem of individuals, we can help them overcome behavioral problems such as unhealthy eating habits.[34] Integral to the self-esteem movement was concern that ethnic minorities are particularly vulnerable to suffer low self-esteem, and ethnic minority self-esteem also became a major research topic.[35]

---

[33] See readings in Mecca et al. (1989).

[34] For example, see O'Dea and Abraham (2000).

[35] Porter and Washington (1993).

Orth and Robins propose that self-esteem has become "…arguably the most widely studied variable in the behavioral and social sciences…"[36] One implication of the self-esteem movement is that efforts should be made to boost the self-esteem of ethnic groups.

The multiculturalism hypothesis implies that in terms of policy, the government should help each heritage group to feel pride and confidence in its own history and traditions. In turn, because individuals feel pride and confidence in their own identities, they will be open and accepting toward outgroups who have different cultural traditions and histories. The support of the government would be equal across all groups because, according to Canadian multiculturalism (which sets the standard and example, being the first federally endorsed multiculturalism policy), there is no official culture and no "…ethnic group take precedent over any other."[37]

In the Canadian context, various programs have been adopted to try to help people become confident in their own identities. Most importantly, Canada has a funded government Multiculturalism Program (this was moved to the Department of Canadian Heritage in 2015, and following the October 2019 election, it falls under the responsibility of the Ministry of Diversity and Inclusion and Youth). The Multiculturalism Program promotes a number of activities that sustain and extend diversity. For example, ethnocultural minorities are supported to hold cultural festivities, and also educational activities that help maintain their heritage cultures and languages.

Canada is also spearheading efforts to monitor and assess developments in multiculturalism internationally. The various efforts made by different governments to support multiculturalism are monitored and assessed by the Multicultural Policy Index (MPI), housed in Queen's University, Canada.[38] The MPI monitors and reports on the development of multicultural policies in 21 Western democracies. This enables us to compare the progress of multiculturalism across these 21 societies, and current assessments show that multiculturalism has been gaining strength since the late twentieth century. Thus, despite the so-called backlash against multiculturalism, objective measures show that the multiculturalism movement has become stronger in 21 Western democracies.

---

[36] Orth and Robins (2022, p. 5).

[37] Trudeau (1971/1992, p. 281).

[38] Multiculturalism Policies Index (2006–2020).

The Government Should Support Multiculturalism in Both the Public and Private Sectors

The value system supporting multiculturalism has become extensive and pervasive in many Western and also some non-Western countries.[39] The general expectation is that the government should support multiculturalism in both private and public sectors. This trend can be better clarified by reviewing the details of the Multiculturalism Policy Index (MPI), which has been used to assess progress in multiculturalism in 21 Western democracies.[40] As explained below, in most areas progress in multiculturalism has depended on government policies and actions. I begin by reviewing the eight indicators used to make assessments using the Multiculturalism Policy Index, and then I examine progress made by selected countries.

The first indicator integral to the Multiculturalism Policy Index concerns the existence of "Constitutional, legislative or parliamentary affirmation of multiculturalism at the central and/or regional and municipal levels and the existence of a government ministry, secretariat or advisory board to implement this policy in consultation with ethnic communities."[41] This is the most direct check on the official mechanism(s) through which governments do or do not implement multiculturalism. The expectation is that countries that support multiculturalism will have formal government offices devoted to providing this support. Also, the expectation is that this government body will consult directly with ethnic minorities.

Education is seen as the most powerful instrument for governments to socialize the young and teach them to practice multicultural values. Accordingly, the second indicator used in the Multiculturalism Policy Index is "The adoption of multiculturalism in school curriculum."[42] The Expansive influence of multiculturalism is apparent as soon as one enters public schools in many countries, particularly through announcements and slogans of different types declaring that "We Are All Different and Special!" "Everyone is a Star!" and "Celebrate Our Differences!" In line with this, there are special festivals and events (e.g., "African-American month," "Hispanic Heritage month") that in different ways support multiculturalism. An important theme in the multiculturalism curriculum in schools is that each ethnic group is different and has special histories, experiences, talents, and skills that must be valued equally.

Alongside the formal education system, the mass media plays an enormously important role in socializing the young. The role of the mass media is becoming increasingly important with the expansion of electronic communications and the Internet. Accordingly, the third indicator integral to the Multiculturalism Policy Index is "The inclusion of ethnic representation/sensitivity in the mandate of public

---

[39] For example, for a discussion of multiculturalism in Malaysia and Singapore, see Noor and Leong (2013).

[40] Wallace et al. (2021).

[41] Wallace et al. (2021, p. 1).

[42] Wallace et al. (2021, p. 1).

media or media licensing."[43] This index involves two key aspects. The first is ethnic representation in the media: do the people who appear on the media (e.g., television shows, movies) accurately reflect the ethnic mix of the general population in society? The second key aspect of this index is sensitivity to ethnic issues, such as how and in what ways ethnic minorities are represented in the media. For example, ethnic representations in the media should work against rather than endorse negative ethnic stereotypes associated with prejudice and discrimination against minorities.

In many countries that support and practice multiculturalism, schoolchildren have to adhere to dress codes when they attend public (i.e., government) schools. But in some other countries that support multiculturalism, public schools do not have a dress code (I attended schools in England, which had dress codes, but my children attended schools in the United States, which did not have dress codes). School dress codes often forbid at least some aspects of the dress styles of some minorities, and this often includes religious dress. The fourth indicator of the Multiculturalism Policy Index is "Exemptions from dress codes (either by statute or court cases)."[44] The idea here is that religious minorities have the right to be treated differently and to be exempted from adherence to school dress codes, so that they can continue to wear their traditional clothing and insignia.

When immigrants arrive in the adopted land, they still have memories and emotional ties to their countries of birth. Many or all of their families and childhood friends continue to live in the "old country." Electronic communications and contemporary transportation systems mean that robust ties to the old country can now be maintained far more easily for many more years. But in order to take full advantage of opportunities, including the right to vote in political elections, immigrants must become citizens of the adopted country. The connections of immigrants to the old country and community suffer a blow when the law of the adopted land requires that they abandon the citizenship of their country of birth, if they become a citizen of the adopted country. Thus, a fifth indicator of the Multiculturalism Policy Index is that the adopted country "Allows dual citizenship."[45] Through dual citizenship, immigrants retain emotional, cultural, and social ties to both the country of birth and the adopted land.

Minority ethnic groups typically have lower levels of both material and nonmaterial resources, relative to the majority group. This relative lack of resources means that minority ethnic groups are less capable of mobilizing for collective action, as predicted by resource mobilization theory and other theories of collective movements.[46] This means that government support for ethnic group activities is imperative. The sixth indicator of the Multiculturalism Policy Index is "The funding of ethnic group organizations or activities."[47] The government should have an adequate

---

[43] Wallace et al. (2021, p. 2).

[44] Wallace et al. (2021, p. 2).

[45] Wallace et al. (2021, p. 2).

[46] See chapter 2 & 3 in Moghaddam (2024).

[47] Wallace et al. (2021, p. 2).

budget specifically designated for the support of the organizations or activities of different minority ethnic groups.

Most immigrants speak a mother tongue that is different from the official language of the adopted land. These mother tongues help to maintain and perpetuate the heritage cultures of immigrant groups. Even if we do not adhere to a strong version of the Sapir-Whorf hypothesis, according to which our language determines our worldview, it is clear that languages do help to shape at least some aspects of our constructions of the world and sustain our cultures.[48] The death of languages often means the death of the cultures those languages support (as discussed in Chaps. 1 and 2 of this text). Consequently, the survival of languages is essential for the survival of heritage cultures. In line with this, the seventh indicator of the Multiculturalism Policy Index is "The funding of bilingual education or mother-tongue instruction."[49] This funding can be for bilingual schools, or bilingual classes in unilingual schools, or for other special programs designed to successfully pass heritage languages to the next generation of ethnic group members.

Perhaps the most challenging and controversial issue with respect to government-mandated multiculturalism policy concerns the inclusion and representation of ethnic minorities in different governmental and nongovernmental organizations and decision-making bodies. In most countries, ethnic minorities are underrepresented at the higher levels of both government and private sector organizations, and their absence is especially obvious in the higher ranks of organizations in finance, politics, and other key sectors concerned with material resources. This reflects the lower economic wealth and political clout of ethnic minorities, which spills over to other sectors. For example, in hospitals and universities, ethnic minorities are underrepresented among the board of directors, the senior management, and specialized medical doctors and senior professors, but ethnic minorities are overrepresented among the cleaning staff, maintenance workers, and technicians. One solution to this lack of representation at the higher levels of organizations is affirmative action policies that in certain ways target and give priority to ethnic minorities in recruitment and hiring. In line with this, the eighth indicator of the Multiculturalism Policy Index is the country having a program for "Affirmative action for disadvantaged immigrant groups."[50] However, the Supreme Court of the United States has ruled that affirmative actions in higher education are illegal. Obviously, the United States does not meet this eighth requirement of the Multiculturalism Policy Index.

Applying the Multiculturalism Policy Index to 21 Western democracies, Rebecca Wallace and colleagues concluded that Australia has the highest rank, meeting all eight indices (attaining a score of 8 out of 8), followed by Canada, Finland, and Sweden as equal second (each attaining a score of 7 out of 8). The rankings of the other top countries were New Zealand (fifth, with 6.5 out of 8) and the United Kingdom (sixth, with 6 out of 8). The lowest ranked countries were Japan (21st,

---

[48] See the readings in Pinxten (2011) for critical discussions of the Sapir-Whorf hypothesis.
[49] Wallace et al. (2021, pp. 2–3).
[50] Wallace et al. (2021, p. 3).

with 0 out of 8), Denmark (equal 18th, with 1 out of 8), the Netherlands (equal 18th, with 1 out of 8), and Switzerland (equal 18th, with 1 out of 8). The United States was equal tenth (with 3.5 out of 8).

The assessment of different countries using the Multiculturalism Policy Index is highly relevant, because integral to multiculturalism is the idea that the central government should support multiculturalism through official policies. Although there has been some backlash against multiculturalism, especially associated with right-wing populist movements, there are sectors of societies that continue to support multiculturalism—such as ethnic minorities and people of all ethnicities with high levels of education.[51]

Concluding Comment

The multiculturalism movement is powerful and pervasive, encompassing both government and private sector programs in many different Western and non-Western societies. Despite backlash involving a variety of critics, multiculturalism continues to influence policies in many domains, especially education. In practice, multiculturalism has not become influential in all major sectors. For example, as Ruth Fincher and colleagues argue, city planners now have to engage with and help to shape multiculturalism in everyday life.[52] Architects and city planners have to grapple with multiculturalism as they plan and design. Similarly, healthcare professionals, the police and security forces, and marketing and sales forces—everyone—face the challenge of working in multicultural contexts. However, underlying multiculturalism are a number of foundational assumptions, which are critically assessed in the next chapter.

References

Berry, J. W. (2023). The search for some general psychological principles for improving intercultural living in plural societies. *Psychology and Developing Societies, 35,* 278–301.

Berry, J. W., Kalin, R., & Taylor, D. M. (1977). *Multiculturalism and ethnic attitudes in Canada.* Supply and Services Canada.

Bobowik, M., Benet-Martinez, V., & Repke, L. (2022). "United in diversity": The interplay of social network characteristics and personality in predicting outgroup attitudes. *Group Processes & Intergroup Relations, 25,* 1175–1201.

---

[51] For example, regarding ethnic minority support for multiculturalism, see Moghaddam and Breckenridge (2010); regarding education level and support for multiculturalism, see Hooghe and de Vroome (2015).

[52] Fincher et al. (2014).

Bonilla, T., & Tillery, A. B. (2020). Which identity frames boost support for an mobilization in the #BlackLivesMatter movement? An experimental test. *American Political Science Review, 114*, 947–962.

Brown, R. (2020). The social identity approach: Appraising the Tajfelian legacy. *British Journal of Social Psychology, 59*, 5–25.

Cohen-Almagor, R. (2022). *The republic, secularism, and security: France versus the burqa and the niqab*. Springer Briefs in Political Science.

Fincher, R., Iveson, K., Leitner, K., & Preston, V. (2014). Planning in the multicultural city: Celebrating diversity or reinforcing differences? *Progress in Planning, 92*, 1–55.

Flynn, F. J. (2005). Having an open mind: The impact of openness to experience on interracial attitudes and impression formation. *Journal of Personality and Social Psychology, 88*, 816–826.

Fominaya, C. F. (2010). Collective identity in social movements: Central concepts and debates. *Sociology Compass, 4*(6), 393–404.

Gaudette, T., Scrivens, R., Davies, G., & Frank, R. (2021). Upvoting extremism: Collective identity formation and the extreme right on Reddit. *New Media & Society, 23*, 3491–3508.

Gomez, L. E., & Bernet, P. (2019). Diversity improves performance and outcomes. *Journal of the National Medical Association, 111*, 383–392.

Goethe, E. V., & Colina, C. M. (2018). Taking advantage of diversity within the classroom. *Journal of Chemical Education, 95*, 189–192.

Hong, L., & Page, S. E. (2004). Groups of diverse problem solvers can outperform groups of high-ability problem solvers. *Proceedings of the National Academy of Sciences, 101*, 16385–16389.

Hooghe, M., & de Vroome, T. (2015). How does the majority public react to multiculturalist policies? A comparative analysis of European countries. *American Behavioral Scientist, 59*(6), 747–768.

John, O. P. (2021). History, measurement, and conceptual elaboration of the Big-Five trait taxonomy: The paradigm matures. In O. P. John & R. W. Robins (Eds.), *Handbook of personality: Theory and research* (pp. 35–82). The Guilford Press.

Longva, A. N., & Roald, A. S. (Eds.). (2012). *Religious minorities in the Middle East: Domination, self-empowerment, accommodation*. Brill.

Mansfield, N. (2000). *Subjectivity: Theories of the self from Freud to Haraway*. Routledge.

McCreight, J. (2016). *Celebrating diversity through language study: A new approach to grammar lessons*. Heinemann.

McLaren, P. (2018). *Revolutionary multiculturalism: Pedagogies of dissent for the new millennium* (2nd ed.). Routledge.

Mecca, A., Smelser, N. J., & Vasconcellos, J. (Eds.). (1989). *The social importance of self-esteem*. University of California Press.

Moghaddam, F. M. (2008). *Multiculturalism and intergroup relations: Implications for democracy in global context*. American Psychological Association Press.

Moghaddam, F. M. (2023). *How psychologists failed: We neglected the poor and minorities, favored the rich and privileged, and got science wrong*. Cambridge University Press.

Moghaddam, F. M. (2024). *The psychology of revolution*. Cambridge University Press.

Moghaddam, F. M., & Breckenridge, J. (2010). Homeland security and support for multiculturalism, assimilation, and omniculturalism policies among Americans. *Homeland Security Affairs, 4*, 1–14.

Multiculturalism Policy Index. (2006–2020). http://www.queensu.ca/mcp/

Noor, N. M., & Leong, C. H. (2013). Multiculturalism in Malaysia and Singapore: Contesting models. *International Journal of Intercultural Relations, 37*, 714–726.

O'Dea, J. A., & Abraham, S. (2000). Improving the body image, eating attitudes, and behaviors of young male and female adolescents: A new educational approach that focuses on self-esteem. *International Journal of Eating Disorders, 28*, 43–57.

Orth, U., & Robins, R. W. (2022). Is high self-esteem beneficial? Revisiting a classic question. *American Psychologist, 77*, 5–17.

Pinxten, R. (Ed.). (2011). *Universalism versus relativism in language and thought: Proceedings of a colloquium on the Sapir-Whorf hypothesis*. Walter de Gruyter.

Polletta, F., & Jasper, J. M. (2001). Collective identity and social movements. *Annual review of Sociology, 27*(1), 283–305.

Porter, J. R., & Washington, R. E. (1993). Minority identity and self-esteem. *Annual Review of Sociology, 19*, 139–161.

Putnam, R. D. (2007). E Pluribus Unum: Diversity and community in the twenty-first century: The 2006 Johan Skytte Lecture. *Scandinavian Political Studies, 30*, 137–174.

Shorten, A. (2022). *Multiculturalism: The political theory of diversity today*. Polity Press.

Simon, B., Loewy, M., Stürmer, S., Weber, U., Freytag, P., Habig, C., Kampmeier, C., & Spahlinger, P. (1998). Collective identification and social movement participation. *Journal of Personality and Social Psychology, 74*, 646–658.

Sparkman, D. J., Eidelman, S., & Blanchar, J. C. (2017). Multicultural experiences reduce prejudice through personality shifts in openness to experience. *European Journal of Social Psychology, 46*, 840–853.

Tajfel, H. (Ed.). (1978). *Differentiation between social groups: Studies in the social psychology of intergroup relations*. Academic Press.

Taylor, C. (1992). *Multiculturalism and "the politics of recognition"*. Princeton University Press.

Thomas, E. F., Zubielevitch, E., Sibley, C. G., & Osborne, D. (2020). Testing the social identity model of collective action longitudinally and across structurally disadvantaged and advantaged groups. *Personality and Social Psychology Bulletin, 46*, 823–838.

Trudeau, O. E. (1992). Statement by the prime minister in the house of commons, October 8, 1971. In *Multiculturalism in Canada: The challenge of diversity* (pp. 281–283). Nelson Canada. Original work published 1971.

Wallace, R., Tolley, E., & Vonk, M. (2021). *Multiculturalism policy Index: Immigrant minority policies*. Queen's University.

Walzer, M. (1997). *On toleration*. Yale University Press.

Womack, D. F. (2020). Christian communities in the contemporary Middle East: An introduction. *Exchange, 49*, 189–213.

Woodley, X., Hernandez, C., Parra, J., & Negash, B. (2017). Celebrating differences: Best practices in culturally responsive teaching online. *TechTrends, 61*, 470–478.

Chapter 6
Rethinking Multiculturalism

In 2010 the political leaders of the United Kingdom (UK), France, and Germany all declared that multiculturalism has failed.[1] These declarations came in the midst of heated public debates and critical research discussions about multiculturalism.[2] Despite being highly influential in education, government, business, and other key domains, and despite its popularity among ethnic minorities, more educated people of all ethnicities, among other groups, it has become apparent that multiculturalism suffers profound shortcomings. Some of these shortcomings have been discussed in the various critical assessments that have taken place about multiculturalism in the early twenty-first century.[3] For example, although multiculturalism receives robust support from minority groups, majority groups tend to feel it excludes them. My goal here is to systematically review a more complete list of serious shortcomings underlying multiculturalism from the perspective of psychological science. These shortcomings are discussed in order based on their conceptual connections, rather than in terms of their importance.

Treatment of Culture as Discrete, Independent, and Stable

Multiculturalism supports the identification, retention, and celebration of cultures, particularly those associated with ethnicities. Thus, integral to multiculturalism have been programs in schools, such as "African-American month," "Hispanic month," and "Asian-American month." An assumption underlying this perspective is that cultures are discrete, independent, and stable. Opposed to this, a number of historians, social scientists, and others have argued that cultures are in important and consequential ways overlapping, fluid, and constantly changing.[4]

---

[1] Chin (2017).

[2] For example, see Kelly (2002) and Coulthard (2014).

[3] For example, see Cobb et al. (2020).

[4] Related to this are explorations of polyculturalism; see discussions by the historian Prashad (2001), and related social science research (Osborn et al., 2020).

© The Author(s), under exclusive license to Springer Nature Switzerland AG 2024
F. M. Moghaddam, *The Psychology of Multiculturalism, Assimilation,
and Omniculturalism*, SpringerBriefs in Psychology,
https://doi.org/10.1007/978-3-031-62597-8_6

The idea that cultures are historically interconnected in deep ways calls into question the multiculturalism emphasis on celebrating cultural differences. If we accept the interconnected nature of cultures, which of their differences should we celebrate? We must keep in mind that such differences are not static—they have evolved over time and will continue to change. Given that cultures are continually changing, which version of a culture and cultural differences should we celebrate? Instead of differences, why should we not celebrate what humans have in common (as is proposed by omniculturalism, presented in greater detail in Chap. 7 in this text)?

Also, by supporting the maintenance and celebration of cultures as distinct entities, are we not in danger of imprisoning individuals within cultural straightjackets? Just because individuals on the basis of phenotypic characteristics are seen by others as being African America, Hispanic, or Asian American in ethnicity, must they then be expected to maintain and celebrate African-American culture, Hispanic culture, and Asian-American culture, respectively? Perhaps some 10-year-old children are attracted most strongly to what they see as African-American culture, despite being seen by teachers and others at their school as *not* belonging to the African-American group. Perhaps they prefer to celebrate the culture of a group to which others do not assign them. In response, defenders of multiculturalism have argued that despite being overlapping and changing, cultures are distinct, and the collective rights of minorities call for the protection of minority cultures.[5]

The Shortcomings of Relativism Underlying Multiculturalism

Multiculturalism treats all cultures as equal. For example, this "equal treatment" is part of the original statement on multiculturalism from Prime Minister Pierre Trudeau of Canada in 1971.[6] As we discussed in Chap. 1, this represents a relativist as opposed to a universalist position, and proposes that the characteristics of cultures are to be judged according to the value systems within the cultures themselves, not by outsiders using criteria from outside the group being judged. On the surface, this relativist approach seems to favor minorities, because they are given the right to uphold and practice their own culture, their own ways of doing things. Also, minorities are evaluated according to criteria within their own cultures. However, on closer inspection, it turns out that a relativist approach works against minorities (as well as the rest of society, ultimately). This is a point already touched on in Chap. 1 of this book, but now I want to explore further how a relativist position works against minorities within minorities, such as women in minority cultures that discriminate against women. Unfortunately, in many cases such discrimination is extremely harsh, unfair, and backward.

---

[5] For example, see Kymlicka (1995).

[6] Trudeau (1992).

Not surprisingly, some of the earliest and most strident critics of multiculturalism were feminists. This is because women often represent a minority within minorities, and suffer severe discrimination because of biases integral to some minority
cultures. Related to this, Ayelet Shachar had argued that:

> Multiculturalism accommodation presents a problem…when pro-identity group policies
> aimed at leveling the playing field between minority communities and the wider society
> unwittingly allow systematic maltreatment of individuals within the accommodated group –
> an impact which in certain cases is so severe that it can nullify these individual's citizenship
> rights. Under such conditions, well-meaning accommodation by the state may leave mem-
> bers of minority groups vulnerable to severe injustice within the group, and may, in effect,
> work to reinforce some of the most hierarchical elements of a culture.[7]

What Shachar refers to as the reinforcement of "hierarchical elements of a culture"
sometimes works in subtle and indirect ways, but they can also work in brutal and
direct ways.

For example, consider the tradition practiced in many Muslim countries that
women cannot serve as law court judges.[8] This "tradition" was enforced rigidly after
the 1979 revolution in Iran, which brought into power religious extremist followers
of Ayatollah Ruhollah Khomeini (1902–1989). During my time in postrevolution
Iran, when I asked supporters of the fundamentalist regime why women should not
serve as judges, their answers included the ideas that "women are too emotional in
their judgements; they are not able to judge objectively" and "a judge is like a
guardian, but throughout their lives women are under the guardianship of men (their
fathers, or brothers, or husbands, or sons) and are not able to serve as guardians of
others." This is just one of many, many examples (including forced hijab for women
and men having the right to practice polygamy) one could give of how traditional
practices in Islamic societies discriminate against women. But from a relativist perspective, these practices must only be evaluated within the value system of the culture in which they exist. That is, for example, the third-class treatment of women in
Iran by the mullahs (and in Afghanistan by the Taliban) can only be evaluated within
Iran (and Afghanistan), and not according to universal rights. Not surprisingly,
Iranian fundamentalists have been very supportive of multiculturalism, arguing that
each society has the right to practice its own way of life, free from interference from
outsiders.[9]

It is in this context that we can better appreciate Shachar's comment (quoted
above) that "…well-meaning accommodation by the state may leave members of
minority groups vulnerable to severe injustice within the group." When, through
multiculturalism, the government in a country such as Canada supports minority
cultures, there is a danger that it is supporting the continuation of cultural practices

---

[7] Shachar (2001, pp. 2–3).

[8] Cardinal (2010) provides an insightful discussion of this limitation faced by women in the context
of Syria.

[9] For example, there was an international meeting in Tehran in support of the multiculturalism
approach, the *International Conference on Multiculturalism and Global Community*, Tehran, Iran.
24–27 July, 2010.

that work against some minority members, such as women. It could be argued that national and international laws are there to protect minorities within minorities. However, particularly in the context of multicultural societies where differences are officially celebrated, cultural practices can function in extremely subtle ways that sometimes continue unfair practices informally, despite being against formal national and/or international law. For example, cultural practices can continue in subtle and hidden ways to discriminate against women within families, even though formal national and international law might forbid such practices.

Motivation to Retain and Share the Heritage Culture

In the 1980s, after I left Iran, I was very fortunate to find an academic home at McGill University, Canada, and to collaborate with Don Taylor (1943–2021), a gregarious, brilliant, and genuinely generous larger-than-life Canadian. As new arrivals in Canada, my wife and I had a fairly standard view of the immigrant experience: we expected there would be years of hardship and feelings of being outsiders, followed by gradual progress and a feeling of belonging, of being accepted as part of our host society. This standard view was constantly being reinforced by others, particularly more established immigrants who told us that after the first 10 years or so, we would feel more at home. It came as a surprise to me, then, to discover that the research I was conducting with Don Taylor at McGill contradicted this cosey picture. For example, in a study of visible minority immigrant women, we found that the longer these women lived in Canada, the *less* they felt at home.[10] At first, I was so puzzled about this result that I thought we had coded our data incorrectly. But no, after many checks, and after more interviews with visible minority immigrant women, I realized that the pattern of results we had found was valid and stable. This led me to rethink how different groups of immigrants and refugees experience multiculturalism and the opportunity to retain and celebrate their cultures.

Imagine you are a White Christian British immigrant to North America. Your mother tongue is English, your religion is the majority group religion, you look like the White majority group in your adopted land, and you are happy to celebrate and share your British cultural heritage. It makes good sense to assume that the longer you live in North America, the more you feel at home. Now, imagine an alternative scenario: you are a Black female Muslim Nigerian immigrant to North America. You were forced by family members to wear the hijab and undergo female circumcision.[11] In addition, like the visible minority women in our research, you may feel there is discrimination against your group in your adopted land. Consequently, you might not want to retain and celebrate your cultural heritage because you feel that your cultural heritage discriminates against females and you do not want to pass it

---

[10] Moghaddam and Taylor (1987).

[11] See Abiodun et al. (2011) for an account of female circumcision in Nigeria.

on to the next generation. Second, you feel that retaining and celebrating your cultural heritage does not help you integrate and make progress in your adopted land.

Underlying multiculturalism is the assumption that minority group members are motivated to retain and celebrate their heritage cultures. This may well be the case for some groups (such as the White Christian British Immigrant I refer to above), but for others—and particularly for minorities within minorities who feel subjugated within their own heritage cultures, such as women in Islamic societies influenced by fundamentalism—the motivation is sometimes to escape the heritage culture, rather than to maintain and celebrate it. Why would you celebrate a culture that treats you as a third-class citizen? Especially from the perspective of minorities within minorities, the assumption that ethnic minority members actually want to retain their heritage cultures is highly questionable.

The Celebration of Intergroup Differences

A central feature of multiculturalism is the celebration of intergroup differences. This has led to school programs in which children research the roots of their own and other ethnic groups, and search for how groups are different.[12] Of course, children are encouraged to show creativity and innovation to find new bases on which intergroup differences can be celebrated. The goal of these school projects it to discover and celebrate differences between groups, and so the reward system influences children to keep focused on uncovering differences (rather than similarities). For example, when interviewing their older relatives about their family stories, their ways of life, their traditions, and so on, the underlying question guiding the children is: "How are we different from other groups?" "How can I find intergroup differences to celebrate?" The question is not: "How are we similar to everyone else?" Or "What are the shared characteristics that we can celebrate?"

The priority given by multiculturalism to intergroup differences also influences behavior patterns in the larger society. This pattern follows what the historian Eric Hobsbawm (1917–2012) has explored as "inventing tradition," where some kind of behavior—typically in the form of a custom—is invented at a recent time and spreads in a group, but is treated as if it has deep historical roots and is ancient.[13] An example of this is Kwanzaa, "Designed to resemble the ritual at an African harvest festival,"[14] which is positioned as being ancient but was actually created in 1966 in the United States (not in Africa). Let me stress that Kwanzaa is not unusual; it is an example of an invented tradition, and invented traditions are common to all human

---

[12] Wessinger (1994, p. 63).

[13] For example, see Hobsbawm's (1999) discussions of the production of traditions in Europe in the decades around the late 1800s and early 1900s.

[14] Pleck (2001, p. 3).

groups.[15] There are other examples of invented tradition that are far less visible than Kwanzaa, but in some respects even more powerful in how they influence the behavior of people of different ethnicities. This includes the invention of myths about the founding of the United States and the Western expansion of American society to "tame the wilderness."[16]

Sidetracking of Minorities, Especially in Education

Multiculturalism is about maintaining and celebrating cultural differences, but can (unintentionally) perpetuate the subtle but powerful ways in which cultural stereotypes negatively influence behavior. The message of multiculturalism, especially loud and far-reaching in education, is that "each group is different." The subtle implication is that groups can be successful in their different ways, along different paths. For example, while some groups are more likely to find success in sports or other domains (such as show business), other groups are more likely to find success through doing well in schoolwork and standardized testing.

The statistics on the level of educational success of each ethnic group provides a clear and fairly consistent picture.[17] Supporters of multiculturalism also agree on how well different groups do in education. For example, Hannah Birnbaum and colleagues sum up the trends in this way, "…African American, Latino, and Native American students…obtain lower grades and drop out of college at higher rates than their White and Asian counterparts."[18] But there is disagreement about the solution. While some researchers argue for an even more expansive implementation of multicultural programs in education, I am among those who caution that the "celebrating differences" approach of multiculturalism has in some cases served to distract ethnic minorities away from engaging fully with traditional academic learning.

There is a danger that the "celebrating differences" approach is resulting in "bookish learning" being associated more with some ethnic groups (e.g., Asians and Whites) and less with others (e.g., African Americans and Latinos). Related to this is the discussion about some minorities being accused of "acting White" when they are seen as being "too bookish."[19] And at the same time, there is a danger that the path to success through sport is more associated with some ethnic groups (e.g., African Americans) than some others (e.g., Asians). The result in some cases can be lower commitment, and a sense that "bookish learning" is not for my group.

---

[15] For example, see Maguire (2011) on how invented traditions associated with sport are shaping national identities across the globe.

[16] Bowden (1992).

[17] See de Brey et al. (2019).

[18] Birnbaum et al. (2021, p. 751).

[19] See Ogbu and Davis (2003), and the related discussion of Fryer Jr and Torelli (2010).

An important question is: "How do these associations come about?" The answer is that they come about through cultural norms, made effective by extremely subtle verbal and nonverbal communications. For example, in discussing the lack of ethnic minorities in science, David Asai points to the role of "…microaffirmations – the subtle kindness cues communicated through tone of voice and the practice of listening to understand…."[20] These include microaffirmations that make some individuals feel comfortable on a football field, but not in a science laboratory.

However, in this discussion I am pointing to far more than the subtleties of inter-individual communication. Rather adopting a "societies to cells" approach,[21] I am highlighting the role of collective culture and the values and stereotypes "out there" in society, and how this collective culture infiltrates the microlevel of inter-individual communications (e.g., in science classes) to nudge students in one direction rather than in other directions. Multiculturalism has become part of our collective culture, and my contention is that in some cases it influences students to see "bookishness" as less applicable to their group.

I am not contending that the subtle messages about celebrating group differences, and each group having a different path to success, account for all the ethnic group disparities in school test scores. Other factors also play an important role. For example, as I have argued elsewhere and as demonstrated by extensive research evidence, wealth disparities are in part responsible for ethnic group disparities in test scores.[22] Family wealth is still the best predictor of the university students will graduate from. However, the role of multiculturalism is not negligible, and my contention is that at present this role tends to distract at least some ethnic minorities from traditional school studies and redirect at least some of them to alternative nonacademic routes, particularly sports.

The Multiculturalism Hypothesis

> National unity, if it is to mean anything in the deeply personal sense, must be founded on confidence in one's own individual identity; out of this can grow respect for others and a willingness to share ideas, attitudes and assumptions.[23]

The multiculturalism hypothesis is closely associated with the official statement (quoted above and discussed in Chap. 5) from Canadian Prime Minister Pierre Trudeau (1919–2000), the father of Prime Minister Justin Trudeau, introducing the policy of multiculturalism in the Canadian Parliament in 1971. The basic idea is that when people are confident in their own ethnic identity, they will be more open and

---

[20] Asai (2020, p. 755).

[21] Moghaddam (2023).

[22] See Barrett et al. (2021), Moghaddam (2022), Reardon and Kalogrides (2019), and Reardon et al. (2022).

[23] Trudeau (1971/1992, p. 281).

accepting toward other ethnic groups, and this seems to make good sense—if we assume intergroup relations is shaped by rational processes (which, in many situations, it is not). The policy implications of this idea have been taken to mean that governments should help ethnic groups feel confident in their own identities, because (it is assumed) this will lead them to be more open and accepting toward others. However, despite seeming to represent a commonsense perspective, there is profound disagreement about the validity of this approach at both the theoretical and empirical levels.

Moreover, the multiculturalism hypothesis lumps both minority and majority groups together, and assumes that the relationship between confidence in one's own identity and behavior toward outgroups is the same for both ethnic minorities and for majority groups. As we shall see, this is a questionable assumption and a serious shortcoming of the multiculturalism hypothesis. The behavior of majority and minority groups is in important ways very different in this area. This difference arises in part from majority and minority ethnic groups having different amounts of power and wealth, and subsequently different kinds of impacts as *sources* of intergroup discrimination—an issue I expand on later in this section.

Historically, most researchers have adopted the pessimistic assumption that ingroup love is associated with outgroup hate.[24] Sigmund Freud (1856–1939) is probably the most influential researcher in this tradition.[25] Freud argued that libidinal (emotional) ties within a group can be both positive and negative. In order to improve group functioning, effective leaders act to redirect negative emotions outward onto dissimilar outgroups. In this way, only positive emotional ties remain inside the ingroup. This idea of displacement influenced a tradition of research on the relationship between frustration (negative emotion) and aggression: the idea that the experience of frustration within a group, because of economic depression, for example, can lead to aggression being displaced onto a target external to the group—usually a weak target that is not actually responsible for the experience of frustration.[26] Along the same lines, William Sumner (1840–1910) pioneered research related to *ethnocentrism*, applying one's own group standards to evaluate other groups, which has implicitly and explicitly endorsed the idea that ingroup love is associated with outgroup hate.[27] Seminal research on the authoritarian personality in the immediate post-Second World War period also endorses the pessimistic, ethnocentrism perspective that ingroup love is associated with outgroup hate.[28]

Social identity theory, the most influential modern theory of intergroup relations (as discussed in Chap. 4), has been interpreted by many (but not all) researchers as supporting the idea that ingroup love is associated with outgroup hate. Typical of

---

[24] I am borrowing this phrasing from Brewer (1999).

[25] See in particular Freud (1955, 1957).

[26] Research on frustration-aggression has continued in the twenty-first century, Miller et al. (2003).

[27] Sumner (1906); also see developments of ethnocentrism research reported by LeVine and Campbell (1972) and Balabanis and Siamagka (2022).

[28] See the seminal research on authoritarianism by Adorno et al. (1950).

this interpretation of social identity theory is the following by Marianna Kosic and Corrado Caudek, "The extent to which individuals identify with an ingroup...favors the emergence of ingroup favoritism, and less favorable attitudes toward corresponding outgroups."[29] In line with this interpretation of social identity theory, the minimal group paradigm studies (discussed in Chap. 4) demonstrate that a difference between two groups on the basis of even a trivial criterion can result in bias in favor of the ingroup and against the outgroup. However, some researchers dispute this "pessimistic" interpretation of social identity theory.[30] Historically, there also have been attempts to develop more positive interpretations of the relationship between ingroup love and outgroup attitudes.

Gordon Allport (1897–1967) is the most influential researcher to adopt a more positive view of the relationship between ingroup love and attitudes toward the outgroup.[31] Allport's contention that positivity toward the ingroup does not necessarily lead to negativity toward the outgroup has been well received and further developed by some contemporary researchers, most notably Marilynn Brewer.[32] Allport's contribution is to point to complexities in the relationship between ingroup love and outgroup hate, and this is supported by research that points to the role of additional factors, such as the majority or minority status of the group being examined. A shortcoming of the multiculturalism hypothesis is the assumption that all minority and majority groups need to be supported to feel confidence in their identities, so that (it is assumed) they will become more open and accepting toward outgroups. But an alternative possibility is that the relationship between ingroup love and outgroup hate is different for majority and minority groups.

It is majority group who have the wealth, power, and status to discriminate against minority groups. Minority groups do not have this capability (except for rare cases and in certain small pockets of the economy, the classic being ethnic economic enclaves such as Chinatown[33]). For example, in the United States and Canada, it is White Americans and White Canadians who have the power, resources, and status to discriminate against ethnic minorities. Even if they wanted to, ethnic minorities do not have the capability to discriminate against Whites in the United States and Canada—just as in Europe, ethnic minorities do not have the economic and political capability to discriminate against White Europeans. Minority groups are often found to experience higher levels of ingroup identification and cohesion, because they face discrimination.[34] Consequently, the multiculturalism hypothesis is conceptually flawed, in that it does not differentiate between majority and

---

[29] Kosic and Caudek (2005, p. 103).

[30] See Turner and Reynolds (2004).

[31] Allport (1954).

[32] Brewer (1999).

[33] There is evidence that even in ethnic economic enclaves such as Chinatown, ethnic minorities do not have an advantage (Xie & Gough, 2011).

[34] Duckitt et al. (2005).

minority groups both as sources of discrimination, and also with respect to the consequences that experiencing discrimination has for ingroup identification.

The multiculturalism hypothesis is also questionable when considered in the light of empirical research. First, studies on ingroup identification and outgroup attitudes also point to different patterns of behavior among majority and minority groups.[35] Some evidence suggests that the idea of ingroup love being associated with outgroup hate is more in line with majority rather than minority group behavior. Related to this, direct attempts to measure the relationship between confidence in ingroup identity and attitudes toward outgroups (as proposed by the multiculturalism hypothesis) have resulted in ambiguous findings.[36]

Historical evidence also casts doubt on the multiculturalism hypothesis. There are many historical examples of groups that have expressed great confidence in their own identities, but also showed extreme discrimination, hostility, and outright violence against outgroups. In recent times we could cite the example of the Nazis. Hitler's claim that the Third Reich would last a thousand years suggests great confidence in his group and a sense of superiority on the world stage. But this confidence did not lead to the acceptance of outgroups—very much the opposite.

Of course, it could be claimed that the Nazis, White nationalists, Islamic fundamentalists, and other such groups who express great confidence in their own identities but also show hostility and violence against outgroups are actually weak and lacking in confidence at a deeper level. This line of argument could be supported by differentiating between healthy and unhealthy (narcissistic) types of group identity, and claiming that only healthy group identification leads to positive attitudes toward outgroups.[37] However, in practice this interpretation becomes tautological: whenever a group shows confidence in its own identity and is accepting toward outgroups, we interpret this as reflecting a healthy group identity. But whenever a group shows confidence in its own identity and is hostile toward outgroups, we interpret this as reflecting an unhealthy group identity. In other words, we interpret group identity as healthy or unhealthy, depending on which interpretation will support our argument. Clearly, this is not a valid approach.

Elite Members of Minorities Defend Multiculturalism Out of Self-Interest

Multiculturalism has greatly benefitted elite members of minority communities. These elites are now well established in politics, business, sports, entertainment, science, education, and just about all the most important sectors of society. In politics, these elites have a lot of clout because they seem to be able to deliver votes

---

[35] Kosic and Caudek (2005); Verkuyten (2005).

[36] Lambert et al. (1986).

[37] For example, see de Zavala et al. (2013).

from their ingroup members in support of (or opposition to) particular candidates. For example, in the United States, "the Black vote" and the "Hispanic vote" can decide the outcome of presidential elections, and elite African Americans and Hispanics can be highly influential in how these minorities vote.[38] The visibility of elite minorities in politics and other sectors is taken as a signal that, first, society has become an open meritocracy with circulation of talent and, second, anyone with the necessary abilities, motivation, and other individual characteristics can make it.[39] In essence, elite minorities serve as tokens to endorse the idea that the current system works and minority interests are adequately represented—and if minority group members are unsuccessful, it is because of something lacking within these *individuals*.[40]

It is assumed that part of the representation of minority interests include strong defense of multiculturalism. This happens in all sectors, in obvious and sometimes in less obvious ways. For example, an obvious way in which multiculturalism is defended is in the establishment of "diversity/inclusion" or multiculturalism units as a formal part of organizations, particularly in government and education sectors. In just about every university, there are now "diversity" units, supposedly represent-ing the interests of minorities. In practice, however, these units represent the inter-ests of elites within minorities. The university in which I work is no exception: Georgetown University ranks extremely low in economic diversity, yet has a large unit (supposedly) representing minority interests.[41] The financially poor are obvi-ously not part of this program.

But there are also more subtle ways in which multiculturalism is defended. For example, most political, social, and psychological science journals include mem-bers of minority groups in their editorial and manuscript reviewing system. When a journal receives a manuscript that is in some way related to diversity and multicul-turalism, the manuscript tends to be directed to be reviewed and/or edited by the "representative" minority scholar(s) working within the journal network. These minority scholars are part of elites within minorities. Manuscripts tend to be reviewed under the assumption that defending multiculturalism is synonymous with defending minority group interests. The results are harsh reviews for journal and books manuscripts that cast a light on the negative aspects of multiculturalism. The underlying assumption in these processes is that minority elites are serving the interests of minority non-elites—which is far from the case.

But in practice, the interests of minority elites tend to be very different from the non-elite minority group members. The only thing elite minority individuals have in common with financially poor minority individuals is symbolic characteristics, such

---

[38] The most obvious recent example is the vote of African Americans in the 2008 US presidential elections, in support of Barack Obama (Philpot et al., 2009).

[39] For a discussion of the importance of this perception of the system being open, see Moghaddam (2008, pp. 69–70).

[40] Grant (2017) provides a general discussion of tokenism.

[41] For university rankings on economic diversity, see https://www.nytimes.com/interac-tive/2023/09/11/upshot/college-income-lookup.html.

as the color of their skins. In most other respects, including in terms of their economic interests, elite minorities and non-elite minorities have very little in common. Multiculturalism has brought material resources and status benefits to minority elites; they often serve as the token successes that prove the system is open and meritocratic. However, multiculturalism has brought few benefits of actual substance to non-elite minorities.

Diversion from Economic Inequalities and Poverty

Multiculturalism draws our attention to cultural and ethnic differences, and distracts us from wealth differences, which are growing and far more consequential and important.[42] In particular, multiculturalism distracts from the plight of the poor, who belong to all ethnicities (including Whites) and are suffering both in terms of their objective material conditions and their subjective experiences of relative deprivation.[43] The celebration of ethnicities and cultures as supposedly equal is a distraction from increasingly unequal wealth disparities and the concentration of wealth in fewer and fewer hands, which ultimately has destructive consequences for all human societies. In societies with more extreme wealth disparities, greater relative deprivation and detrimental health is suffered by those with the least amount of wealth—including poor Whites.[44]

Since the 1950s, the scholarship of Simon Kuznets, Anthony Atkinson, Thomas Piketty, and a number of other economists has gradually drawn our attention to the trend of sharply increasing wealth inequalities and wealth concentration.[45] As we discussed in Chap. 4 of this text, the unmistakable trend is that greater and greater wealth is falling into the hands of fewer and fewer individuals, and the bottom 40 percent or so of the wealth population are coming under far greater economic and psychological pressure. Although there are small discrepancies between economists in how they assess the amount of wealth estimated to be in the hands of the superrich, the general agreement among leading experts approaching the topic from different angles is that wealth concentration is extreme and increasing.[46] This trend is more extreme in the United States than in Europe.[47] Also, wealth inequalities are being exacerbated by intergenerational wealth transfers through inheritance and family background differences (such as different education levels of parents).[48]

---

[42] Economic inequality is increasing and very well documented (Deaton, 2023).

[43] For a related discussion, see Fraser and Honneth (2003).

[44] Marmot (2004).

[45] See Atkinson (2015), Kuznets (1953), and Piketty (2014).

[46] For example, see Saez and Zucman (2022) regarding different ways of estimating the wealth of the superrich.

[47] Blanchet and Martinez-Toledano (2023).

[48] Palomino et al. (2022).

Moreover, the benefits of new technologies and automation are going more to the richest people and the workers with higher skills, but less to the poorest group.[49]

The most serious consequences of increasing wealth inequalities manifest themselves in health disparities between people with different levels of wealth. In terms of health, the rich and the superrich live lives that are incomparable to the rest of society, and particularly to the poor. As the epidemiologist Sir Michael Marmot puts it, "It doesn't just feel better at the top. It *is* better. At the top, not only do you live longer but the quality of life is better—you spend more years free from disability…the more deprived people spend more of their shorter lives with 'disability.'"[50] Research shows that health is influenced by complex sets of factors, but growing inequalities in health outcomes are in important ways shaped by wealth inequalities.[51]

Of course, as shown by the research in intersectionality, there is some overlap between ethnicity, gender, and social class.[52] However, this overlap does not negate the fact that multiculturalism focuses on ethnicity and culture, and distracts from growing wealth disparities between the richest and the rest of the population, particularly the poor.

Multiculturalism in a Global Context

Despite the use of the term "post-rights era," we live in an age of rights rather than duties, as discussed in Chap. 1.[53] The rhetoric of rights is overwhelming in the global media. All kinds of rights are being claimed by different groups and individuals, on behalf of themselves and other humans, as well as animals, the environment, and nature.[54] In this era of runaway rights, multiculturalism has also become associated with the rights of ethnic and cultural groups, with the implication that all such groups have equal rights. Multiculturalism in the global context means that if any group sees its rights as being violated anywhere in the world, then it can demand justice, and indeed act to bring about what it views as justice. For example, on February 14, 1989, Ayatollah Ruhollah Khomeini issued a Fatwa ordering Muslims to kill the novelist Salman Rushdie, who had authored *The Satanic Verses*, a novel that Khomeini interpreted as blasphemous. Since the time of the Fatwa, which Khomeini's successor Ayatollah Khamenei (the new "Supreme Leader") subsequently endorsed, Rushdie has been pursued by would-be attackers and has faced

---

[49] de Moll et al. (2024)

[50] Marmot (2015, p. 27).

[51] For examples of new research on the roots of health inequalities, see readings in Kaplan et al. (2017).

[52] For example, see Collins and Bilge (2020).

[53] For "post-rights era," see the example of Lewis et al. (2015). For broader discussions of the psychology of rights and duties, see Finkel and Moghaddam (2005); Moghaddam (2000); Moghaddam et al. (2000).

[54] Canno Pecharroman (2018).

numerous deadly threats. He was stabbed multiple times by a Muslim fanatic on August 12, 2022, while he was giving a speech at the Chautauqua Institute, New York.

The Fatwa against Salman Rushdie highlights the role of relativism, which underlies multiculturalism. A relativist perspective leads to the idea that all groups and cultures have equal value, and the way of life of each group can only be judged according to the values within each group. Was it incorrect for Khomeini to issue the Fatwa against Rushdie, and for Rushdie to be stabbed—not according to the value system of the Islamic extremists ruling Iran. According to them, they have a right to be judged only according to their own value system. These Islamic extremists are highlighting and celebrating intergroup differences, and upholding the right of each group to maintain its own heritage culture.

But Western governments are also deeply influenced by a relativist mindset, so that from the start of the Rushdie affair, they were not able to provide a robust defense of universal human rights, and steadfastly and aggressively stand up for Rushdie's right to free expression. This failure of Western governments to defend the right to free expression against the external threat posed by Khomeini's Fatwa arose in large part from the influence of relativism and multiculturalism *inside* Western societies. With priority being given to the celebration of group differences, and the proposition that all group cultures are equally valuable, Western political leaders became ambivalent about taking decisive action to defend Rushdie. Most Western political leaders looked the other way as Rushdie was forced to go into hiding and his "blasphemous" books were even taken off the shelves of many bookstores in Western countries.

The Rushdie affair represents an extraordinarily powerful episode in the symbolic separation of groups—which is exactly in line with Khomeini's goal of driving a deeper wedge between Western societies and Iran and, if possible, all Islamic societies. From 1979, when Khomeini established an Islamic dictatorship in Iran and spread his brand of radical Islam in Lebanon, Syria, Iraq, Yemen, and some other Islamic societies, he used different radical and violent incidents (including the 1979–1980 invasion of the United States Embassy in Iran and the taking of 52 American diplomats as hostages for 444 days) to try to separate Islamic societies from Western democracies. The way to thwart such schemes, which strove to create further rifts and divisions between groups, is to give highest priority to what all humans have in common, to universal rights and duties, and to international law. Such divisive schemes pursued by extremists are helped when we give priority to differences between groups, most of which are symbolic.

At the same time that symbolic differences, such as the Islamic hijab, are increasingly being used to differentiate and create wider social and psychological gaps between groups, globalization is leading to greater and greater actual similarities between groups. On the one hand, dress codes, food, speech styles, group ceremonies, and other symbolic characteristics of group life are being used to demonstrate and celebrate the distinctiveness of groups. The message is "We are different from you and everybody else, we are special." On the other hand, the globalization of goods and services, and the McDonaldization of societies around the world, has meant that in practice, the lifestyles of people—who are symbolically separated into different groups—have become more similar.[55] Increasingly, the same cars, airplanes, computer models and games, electronic toys, consumer products for the home, building designs, fast-food chains, clothing styles, cosmetics, sports, athletics equipment, and hotel chains, among many other things, are integral to the lives of people who are surrounded by the same material world, but symbolically belong to different groups.

Concluding Comment

Despite the serious and extensive shortcomings of multiculturalism, as I have outlined in this chapter, the fact remains that multiculturalism has robust support among ethnic minorities. There are two main reasons for this. First, multiculturalism brings political and financial benefits for elites within minority ethnic groups, and these elites spearhead national and local support for multiculturalism, influencing non-elite minorities to act against their own interests. Ethnic elites popularize multiculturalism and use the support of non-elite ethnic group members to support their own political careers and business interests. Ethnic elites position themselves as speaking for "their" ethnic groups, both inside and outside governments. In practice, however, ethnic elites act primarily in the interest of rich elites—of all ethnicities.

Correspondingly, in North America, Europe, Australia, New Zealand, and a number of other regions and countries, the White majority group finds it convenient to include ethnic elites in highly visible positions in politics, business, education, and other key sectors, as a way of (at least superficially) including ethnic minorities. When ethnic elites participate in decision-making processes, the claim can be made that ethnic minorities have been included. However, it is not clear that ethnic elites, who tend to be relatively affluent and powerful, reflect the interests of the rest of "their" ethnic groups. In essence, the actual ingroup of ethnic elites is other affluent people of all ethnicities, and their decisions tend to favor other rich people—irrespective of ethnicity. The likes of Rishi Sunak (the UK Prime Minister) serve the interests of other extremely rich people, despite the color of his skin suggesting otherwise.

Through the influence of ethnic elites, multiculturalism has been publicized as being beneficial for ethnic minorities. Ethnic elites have lauded multiculturalism and the celebration of ethnic differences as "a right." Of course, ethnic elites are not alone in propagating this message. In many countries, government agencies have also been charged with disseminating this point of view. Educational institutions and business organizations have followed suit. The consequence of this pattern of behavior is that many ethnic minority members have been persuaded to support the ethnic elites (superficially) representing them, as part of a wider support for

---

[55] Ritzer (2020).

multiculturalism and the celebration of group differences. Unfortunately, the outcome of this process has only benefited ethnic elites (and all elites, more broadly), but not non-elite members of ethnic minorities—who actually have a lot more in common with poor Whites than the elite leadership of "their own" ethnic groups.

References

Abiodun, A. A., Oyejola, B. A., & Job, O. (2011). Female circumcision in Nigeria, prevalence and attitudes. *Centrepoint Journal (Science Edition), 17*, 89–98.

Adorno, T. W., Frenkel-Brunswik, E., Levinson, D. J., & Sanford, B. W. (1950). *The authoritarian personality*. Harper & Row.

Allport, G. W. (1954). *The nature of prejudice*. Addison-Wesley.

Asai, D. J. (2020). Commentary: Race matters. *Cell, 181*, 754–757.

Atkinson, A. (2015). *Inequality: What can be done?* Harvard University Press.

Balabanis, G., & Siamagka, N. T. (2022). A meta-analysis of consumer ethnocentrism across 57 countries. *International Journal of Research in Marketing, 39*, 745–763.

Barrett, N., McEachin, A., Mills, J. N., & Valant, J. (2021). Disparities and discrimination in student discipline by race and family income. *Journal of Human Resources, 56*, 711–748.

Birnbaum, H. J., Stephens, N. M., Townsend, S. S. M., & Hamedani, M. G. (2021). A diversity ideology intervention: Multiculturalism reduces the racial achievement gap. *Social Psychological and Personality Science, 12*, 751–759.

Blanchet, T., & Martinez-Toledano, C. (2023). Wealth inequality dynamics in Europe and the United States: Understanding the determinants. *Journal of Monetary Economics, 133*, 25–43.

Bowden, M. J. (1992). The invention of American tradition. *Journal of Historical Geography, 18*, 3–26.

Brewer, M. B. (1999). The psychology of prejudice: Ingroup love or outgroup hate? *Journal of Social Issues, 55*, 429–444.

Canno Pecharroman, L. (2018). Rights of nature: Rivers that can stand in court. *Resources, 7*, 13–26.

Cardinal, M. C. (2010). Why aren't women sharia court judges? The case of Syria. *Islamic Law and Society, 17*, 185–214.

Chin, R. (2017). *The crisis of multiculturalism in Europe: A history*. Princeton University Press.

Cobb, C. L., Frisby, C., Lilienfeld, S. O., Sanders, G. L., & Schwartz, S. J. (2020). Rethinking multiculturalism: Toward a balanced approach. *American Journal of Psychology, 133*, 275–293.

Collins, P. H., & Bilge, S. (2020). *Intersectionality* (2nd ed.). Polity Press.

Coulthard, G. (2014). *Red skins, white masks: Rejecting the colonial politics of recognition*. University of Minnesota Press.

Deaton, A. (2023). *Economics in America: An immigrant economist explores the land of inequality*. Princeton University Press.

De Brey, C., Musu, L., McFarland, J., Wilkinson-Flicker, S., Diliberti, M., Zhang, A., Branstetter, C., & Wang, X. (2019). *Status and trends in the education of racial and ethnic groups 2018*. National Center for Educational Statistics, U.S. Department of Education. https://nces.ed.gov/programs/raceindicators/indicator_RCB.asp

de Moll, F., Grecu, A. L., & Hadjar, A. (2024). Students' Academic Habitus and Its Relation to Family Capital: A Latent Class Approach to Inequalities among Secondary School Students 1. *Sociological Inquiry, 94*(1), 190–220.

Duckitt, J., Callaghan, J., & Wagner, C. (2005). Group identification and outgroup attitudes in four South African ethnic groups: A multidimensional approach. *Personality and Social Psychology Bulletin, 31*, 633–646.

Finkel, N., & Moghaddam, F. M. (Eds.). (2005). *The psychology of rights and duties: Empirical contributions and normative commentaries*. American Psychological Association Press.

Fraser, N., & Honneth, A. (2003). *Redistribution or recognition? A political-philosophical exchange*. (Trans. J. Golb & J. Ingram). Verso.

Freud, S. (1955). Group psychology and the analysis of the ego. In J. Strachey (Ed.), *The standard edition of the complete psychological works of Sigmund Freud* (Vol. 18, pp. 67–143). Hogarth Press. (Original work published 1921).

Freud, S. (1957). Thoughts for the times on war and death. In J. Strachey (Ed.), *The standard edition of the complete psychological works of Sigmund Freud* (Vol. 14, pp. 271–302). Hogarth Press. (Original work published 1915).

Fryer, R. G., Jr., & Torelli, P. (2010). An empirical analysis of "acting white". *Journal of Public Economics, 94*, 380–396.

Grant, B. (2017). Tokenism. In F. M. Moghaddam (Ed.), *The Sage encyclopedia of political behavior* (Vol. 2, pp. 834–837). Sage.

Hobsbawm, E. (1999). Mass producing traditions: Europe, 1870–1914. In P. Bosswell & J. Evans (Eds.), *Representing the nation: A reader* (pp. 61–86). Routledge.

Kaplan, G. A., Diez Roux, A. V., Simon, C. P., & Galea, S. (Eds.). (2017). *Growing inequality: Bridging complex systems, population health, and health disparities*. Westphalia Press.

Kelly, P. (Ed.). (2002). *Multiculturalism reconsidered: Culture and equality and its critics*. Polity Press.

Kosic, M., & Caudek, C. (2005). Ethnic identification and outgroup attitudes in minority and majority groups. *Review of Psychology, 12*, 103–113.

Kuznets, S. (1953). *Shares of upper income groups in income and savings*. National Bureau of Economic Research.

Kymlicka, W. (1995). *Multicultural citizenship: A liberal theory of minority rights*. Oxford University Press.

Lambert, W. E., Mermegis, L., & Taylor, D. M. (1986). Greek Canadians' attitudes toward own group and other Canadian ethnic groups: A test of the multiculturalism hypothesis. *Canadian Journal of Behavioural Science, 18*, 35–51.

LeVine, R. A., & Campbell, D. T. (1972). *Ethnocentrism: Theories of conflict, ethnic attitudes, and group behavior*. Wiley.

Lewis, N. M., Bauer, G. R., Coleman, T. A., Blot, S., Pugh, D., Fraser, M., & Powell, L. (2015). Community cleavages: Gay and bisexual men's perceptions of gay and mainstream community acceptance of post-AIDS, post-rights era. *Journal of Homosexuality, 62*, 1201–1227.

Maguire, J. A. (2011). Globalization, sport and national identities. *Sport in Society, 14*, 978–993.

Marmot, M. (2004). *The status syndrome: How social standing affects our health and longevity*. Times Books/Henry Holt.

Marmot, M. (2015). *The health gap: The challenge of an unequal world*. Bloomsbury.

Miller, N., Pederson, W. C., Earleywine, M., & Pollock, V. E. (2003). A theoretical model of triggered displaced aggression. *Personality and Social Psychology Review, 7*, 75–97.

Moghaddam, F. M. (2000). Toward a cultural theory of human rights. *Theory & Psychology, 10*, 291–312.

Moghaddam, F. M. (2008). *Multiculturalism and intergroup relations: Implications for democracy in global context*. American Psychological Association Press.

Moghaddam, F. M. (2022). *How psychologists failed: We neglected the poor and minorities, favored the rich and privileged, and got science wrong*. Cambridge University Press.

Moghaddam, F. M. (2023). *How psychologists failed: We neglected the poor and minorities, favored the rich and privileged, and got science wrong*. Cambridge University Press.

Moghaddam, F. M., Slocum, N. R., Finkel, N., & Harré, R. (2000). Toward a cultural theory of duties. *Culture & Psychology, 6*, 275–302.

Moghaddam, F. M., & Taylor, D. M. (1987). The meaning of multiculturalism for visible minority immigrant women. *Canadian Journal of Behavioural Science, 19*, 121–136.

Ogbu, J. A., & Davis, A. (2003). *Black American students in an affluent suburb: A study of academic disengagement*. Routledge.

Osborn, S. J., Sosa, N., & Rios, K. (2020). Perceiving demographic diversity as a threat: Divergent effects of multiculturalism and polyculturalism. *Group Processes & Intergroup Relations, 23*, 1014–1031.

Palomino, J. C., Marrero, G. A., Nolan, B., & Rodriguez, J. G. (2022). Wealth inequality, intergenerational transfers, and family background. *Oxford Economic Papers, 74*, 643–670.

Philpot, T. S., Shaw, D. R., & McGowen, E. B. (2009). Winning the race: Black voter turnout in the 2008 presidential election. *Public Opinion Quarterly, 73*, 995–1022.

Piketty, T. (2014). *Capital in the twenty-first century*. (Trans. A. Goldhammer). The Belknap Press of Harvard University Press.

Pleck, E. (2001). The making of a black nationalist tradition. *Journal of American Ethnic History, 20*, 3–28.

Prashad, V. (2001). *Everybody was Kung Fu fighting: Afro-Asian connections and the myth of cultural purity*. Beacon Press.

Reardon, S. F., & Kalogrides, D. (2019). The geography of racial/ethnic test score gaps. *American Journal of Sociology, 124*, 1164–1221.

Reardon, S. F., Weathers, E. S., Fahle, E. M., Jang, H., & Kalogrides, D. (2022). *Is separate still unequal? New evidence on school segregation and racial academic achievement gaps*. Center for Educational Policy Analysis, Stanford University.

Ritzer, G. (2020). *The McDonaldization of society: Into the digital age* (10th ed.). Sage.

Saez, E., & Zucman, G. (2022). *Top wealth in America: A reexamination*. National Bureau of Economic Research. http://www.nber.org/papers/w30396

Shachar, A. (2001). *Multicultural jurisdictions: Cultural differences and women's rights*. Cambridge University Press.

Sumner, W. G. (1906). *Folkways*. Ginn.

Trudeau, O. E. (1992). Statement by the prime minister in the house of commons, October 8, 1971. In *Multiculturalism in Canada: The challenge of diversity* (pp. 281–283). Nelson Canada. Original work published 1971.

Turner, J. C., & Reynolds, K. J. (2004). The social identity perspective in intergroup relations: Theories, themes, and controversies. In M. B. Brewer & M. Hewstone (Eds.), *Self and social identity* (pp. 259–277). Blackwell.

Verkuyten, M. J. A. M. (2005). Ethnic group identification and group evaluation among minority and majority groups: Testing the multiculturalism hypothesis. *Journal of Personality and Social Psychology, 88*, 121–138.

Wessinger, N. P. (1994). Celebrating our differences—Fostering ethnicity in homogeneous settings. *Journal of Physical Education, 55*, 62–68.

Xie, Y., & Gough, M. (2011). Ethnic enclaves and the earnings of immigrants. *Demography, 48*, 1293–1315.

De Zavala, A. G., Cichocka, A., & Bilewicz, M. (2013). The paradox of in-group love: Differentiating collective narcissism advances understanding of the relationship between in-group and out-group attitudes. *Journal of Personality, 81*, 16–28.

Part II
The Omnicultural Approach as the Best Solution

Government policy has been used to support multiculturalism in some countries (such as Canada) and assimilation in other countries (such as France). However, neither of these paths has been successful in achieving healthy majority-minority relations and adequate economic, political, and educational progress for minorities. Nor has there been more success in countries such as the United States, where the central government plays a less formal role in managing diversity, and market forces are allowed to have more influence. This lack of success is reflected in persistent and serious problems in majority-minority relations, ethnic segregation and discrimination against minorities, the relatively lower achievements of minorities in education, and the lower material wealth and poorer health conditions of minorities. These resilient trends strongly suggest that a new approach is needed to better manage diversity, in a world in which one of the certainties is that many societies will be more diverse tomorrow than they are today. The practical demands of living in societies that are becoming more and more diverse mean that we must give priority to finding better approaches to managing diversity; assimilation and multiculturalism have not worked well enough.

The chapters in in this part critically discuss omniculturalism, and argue it is the best policy for managing diversity. The main characteristics of omniculturalism are introduced in Chap. 7, with attention to conceptual and empirical research that supports this new approach. The topic of Chap. 8 is "our omnicultural world," which explores how in important respects the most valued aspects of human cultures already carry omnicultural themes. In the brief *Afterword*, I argue that omniculturalism is especially suited for helping humankind succeed in meeting our common challenges, including global warming, with a focus on our shared humanity and the vitally important ways in which we humans are all similar. We must seize this opportunity, and move away from prioritizing and celebrating group differences – a path that has resulted in the detrimental trend of manufacturing and exaggerating new intergroup differences that are fictional, but can serve as a basis for rifts and conflicts.

Chapter 7
Introducing Omniculturalism

The point of departure for omniculturalism are three basic ideas: first, human beings are in foundational ways very similar to one another; second, in human relationships we should give priority to similarities rather than differences between people; third, we should acknowledge that humans are to some degree different from one another, but these differences should be treated as secondary and should not be given priority (as happens with multiculturalism). The omnicultural approach is different from *colorblindness*, also referred to as "identity blindness,"[1] which involves ignoring group differences.[2] In contrast, omniculturalism involves, first, *active celebration* of human similarities (which is very different from simply ignoring differences) and, second, acknowledging that there are also some differences between human groups and individuals, and giving a secondary role to these differences.

It is imperative that priority is explicitly given to human similarities during both intergroup and interpersonal interactions. Establishing the many, varied, and important ways in which human beings are similar to one another is a matter for scientific research. Establishing that we *should* give priority to human commonalities rather than to differences between human groups and individuals is a matter for practical reason and the concern of ethics, political science, law, and other research disciplines concerned with how we organize human societies.

Associated with the collective mobilizations of the 1960s was the assumption that minority groups benefit when we give priority to differences rather than to similarities between groups. The priority given to "celebrating our differences" has been associated with identity politics, and attempts to construct and confirm the distinctiveness and even uniqueness of different ethnic groups, including Whites.[3] The

---

[1] Plaut et al. (2018, p. 200). Pecharroman. For earlier discussions of omniculturalism, see Moghaddam (2009, 2012).

[2] Whitley et al. (2023) provide a measure of colorblindness.

[3] For white political identity and mobilization, see Berry et al. (2019).

Civil Rights Movement in the United States is probably the most fruitful and visible part of these collective movements and the social changes they brought about. The idea has been that in order to attain their collective rights and achieve justice, ethnic groups need to construct collective identities that establish how they are different. The implication has been that ethnic groups should take their own independent paths which, it is assumed, are different from the mainstream path.

Ethnic mobilization has been associated with multiculturalism and the celebration of differences, rather than human universals and commonalities. When "rights" have been invoked by, or on behalf of, ethnic minorities, it has often been in relation to the "right to be different." Similarly, "freedom" has often been discussed in relation to the "freedom to go your own way." Along with this priority given to "the right to be different," universal rights and references to human commonalities have been regarded with deep suspicion. This is mainly because historically "universals" have been defined by majority groups and colonial (and more recently, imperial) powers to establish their own (typically ethnocentric) values and criteria as the ones that are correct for all human groups across the globe.

However, just because the idea of universals and human commonalities has been misused in the past by certain colonial and imperial powers does not mean that we should turn our backs to them. Rather, we should improve on our efforts to develop international law in ways that reflects the rights, duties, and interests of all humanity, rather than particular elites. It is a monumental mistake for us to turn our backs on identifying and using human commonalities, just because corrupt powers have misused them in the past. Rather than abandon the principle of universals, particularly in the area of rights, duties, and justice, we must now act to correctly identify, incorporate, and apply universals.

The rights and interests of minorities are best protected through priority being given to how all human beings are foundationally similar to one another, including in the domain of abilities. When we compare humans on basic mental and physical capabilities, it is clear that there are vast overlaps across ethnic groups. Most people of all ethnic groups fall in the central area of the bell curve on measures such as IQ, just as most men and women fall in the same central area. A small number of exceptional individuals are outliers, and they tend to belong to all ethnic and gender groups.[4]

Of course, social class and wealth greatly impact how human potential develops, and this issue has been overlooked. Even though we are all born with similar potential, those born into economically poor families are far less likely to succeed in reaching their potential. For example, the best predictor of educational success is wealth—wealthy families can provide their children with the advanced, intense, and highly expensive training necessary for success in educational tests.[5] Poor families lack the necessary resources and are not able to do this. The result is that ethnic

---

[4] Gould (1996) provides a clear-headed account of grave mistakes made in (mis)measuring IQ and assuming group differences.

[5] See discussions in Moghaddam (2023a).

groups with less wealth do less well in educational testing—as do poor Whites and women from economically deprived families.

But the solution to this is not to give priority to celebrating differences; this takes us backward. Rather, we must refocus on human commonalities and how all humans are born with very similar characteristics and potentials. If they are really given the same material resources and opportunities, the members of different ethnic and gender groups will achieve similar levels of success. This might not happen in the short term, but it will happen in the longer term. The success of women in education demonstrates this, after the opportunities given to women changed to become more similar to men.[6]

Omniculturalism: Goals and Priorities

The first goal of omniculturalism is to give priority to, and to celebrate, those human characteristics that are universal. These characteristics tend also to be continuous across time, and close to what Plato (429?–347 BCE) referred to as "eternal reality" in his writings around 2500 years ago.[7] Of course, we know from research on evolution (and particularly recent developments in epigenetics) that the complex interaction between genetic and environmental characteristics can lead to changes in "human universals," so the match with Plato's "eternal reality" is not perfect.[8] However, although human universals can shift across time, in omniculturalism priority is given to what humans have in common.

The basic principles of omniculturalism are inspired by the ideas of two moral philosophers, the first being Immanuel Kant (1724–1804). The most importance influence of Kant on this discussion is through his concept of *categorical imperative*: "Act only in accordance with that maxim through which you can at the same time will that it become universal law" (G 4:421).[9] Because universal law applies to ourselves as well as everyone else, the implication is that we should treat others as we want to be treated ourselves (I will not delve here into deficiencies in Kant's grand system, because that larger discussion is not relevant to this far narrower discussion of omniculturalism[10]). Of course, integral to the categorical imperative is the necessary inclusion of all humans in the same human group.

This is similar to the *United Nations Declaration of Human Rights* being applicable to all humans, and not just, for example, to those who belong to a particular ethnicity, gender, or nationality. A shortcoming of multiculturalism and priority being given to the "celebration of differences" is that dictator regimes use the "we

---

[6] See the last section in Moghaddam (2023b).

[7] Plato (1987, Book six, 485b).

[8] See Ashe (2021) for a discussion of the epigenetic perspective.

[9] Kant (1785/2002).

[10] For example, see the critical discussion of Kant's possible inconsistencies by O'Neill (1989).

are different" argument to opt out of universal human rights. For example, this morning it was announced that the human rights activist Narges Mohammadi has won the 2023 Nobel Peace Prize. Unfortunately, she is at present in prison in Iran (as are many, many thousands of other Iranian human rights activities, women and men). The mullahs have treated her as a third-class citizen, rejecting the principle that women and men have equal human rights. The dictator regime in Iran argues that "Universal" human rights do not apply to people in Iran, because they are different—and this fits with the "celebrating differences" central to multiculturalism.

Kant's second formula provides direction as to how human commonalities are to be used: "Act so that you use humanity, as much as your own person as in the person of every other, always at the same time as end and never merely as means" (G 4:429). Human commonalities are the essence of being human; they are an end in themselves. In contrast, when people make claims about the special or unique characteristics of their particular group, this is an attempt to use group characteristics as a means—to justify claims about their group being special and superior in some way that justifies their getting a particular (better) outcome relative to others. There are almost endless examples of this, with the most extreme being the twentieth-century Nazis and twenty-first-century White nationalists in North America and Europe, with their claims about their superiority. On the other hand, references to human commonalities depict all humankind as having certain shared characteristics. All human beings are included, because all human beings share these qualities. This represents an end in itself for everyone, not a means to an end only for some people.

John Rawls (1921–2002) is the second moral philosopher who has served as an inspiration for omniculturalism. Rawls invites us to participate in a thought experiment, in which we have some freedom to organize society according to our different values.[11] For example, in this imaginary society, there could be very rich and very poor people, or slave owners and slaves, and men and women could enjoy equality or live as completely unequal groups. But decisions about these groups and their relationships and characteristics will be made under a "veil of ignorance." That is, in making decisions about the roles of different people and the level of equality and inequality among the ethnic, gender, social class, and other groups in society, we will be ignorant of our own group memberships. For example, if we are making decisions about whether there will be slaves and slave owners in our imaginary society, we will not know if we will serve in the role of slave or slave owner. Similarly, when we are deciding about the level of equality and inequality between women and men, and between Blacks and Whites, we will not know if we will be in the role of woman or man, or Black or White. In practice, this "veil of ignorance" results in us treating others as we would want to be treated by them. The overwhelming motivation and goal will be to be treated justly by others, and to treat others justly. Even outside this Rawlsian thought experiment, the justice motive and

---

[11] Rawls (1971).

the need to see the world as just is common to all humans.[12] This is one of the most important human commonalities.

Three Imperatives

In this section I discuss the three imperatives that are at the heart of omnicultural-ism. The first is the *omnicultural imperative*:

> During interactions with other people, under all conditions, first give priority to the charac-teristics you share with other people as members of the human group.

The omnicultural imperative is designed to act as a guide during all interactions with all other humans.[13] The basic idea is that at the forefront, guiding all interac-tions is what we have in common with others. Both when we meet other people for the first time and during our ongoing social relationships, we should be socialized to have this question on our minds: in what ways are these people similar to me? Of course, the answer is that they are similar to me in many important ways. This high-lighting of commonalities, what we share, leads to the inclusion and acceptance of others, rather than their exclusion and rejection. Just as we want to be included and accepted, others also share this desire. This is one of our basic common human characteristics.

Another human characteristic, one that is given secondary importance in omni-culturalism, is the need to belong to groups with some distinct characteristics, as proposed by social identity theory and related research on differentiation.[14] Research points to a tendency for individuals to differentiate themselves from others in cer-tain respects.[15] There is functional value to being different, because it opens up pos-sibilities for finding vacant spaces and available resources not claimed or accessed by our competitors. Beyond this functional, materialist reason for value being given to distinctiveness, "being different" is also valued culturally, as it is associated with authenticity and originality. For example, in art, literature and other creative domains, originality is highly valued.

Omniculturalism provides opportunities for group differences to be given atten-tion through the distinctiveness imperative:

> During interactions with other people, leave some room for, and acknowledge some ways in which, they are different from you.

But the ways in which your group is distinct and different from other groups should not be used as a means to exclude others, because they do not have certain

---

[12] Lerner (1980) discusses the motive to see the world as just as universal and delusional.

[13] There are conditions in which this could be extended to all the natural world, including animals and plants.

[14] Tajfel and Turner (1979); Moghaddam (2008).

[15] Lee et al. (2008).

characteristic(s) or because they have certain characteristics that you do not. Nor should you use this distinctiveness as a means to isolate yourself from others, to put up walls around your group. Above all, differences between groups should be treated as secondary, with primacy being given to similarities across groups. But differences between groups can suggest ways in which some groups can change and improve. In order for such changes to take place, there needs to be communications and sharing across groups with respect to group differences. It is with this point in mind that we can better recognize the role and importance of the sharing imperative:

> Actively reach out to share cultural differences, teaching others about your group's distinct characteristics and also learning about the distinct characteristics of other groups.

In sharing cultural characteristics, two points must be kept in mind. First, the most important group characteristics are common to all groups. These tend to be relatively more stable across time. Second, the characteristics that are distinct to each group tend to be more variable across time. Also, these distinct characteristics can be socially constructed, to create group identities that are in some respects new and that demonstrate how "our group is different from (and better than) your group." This manufacturing of group differences has been enhanced by the value given to the "celebration of differences" as part of the multiculturalism movement. However, omniculturalism requires that, in line with the goal of giving priority to human commonalities, the manufacturing of new differences between groups should be minimized (although it cannot be completely ended).

Psychological Research and Omniculturalism

An extensive body of psychological research casts light on the highly promising avenues for implementing omniculturalism, with positive outcomes. A first body of research suggests possibilities for arriving at a situation where people give priority to human commonalities, despite the historical pervasiveness of ethnocentrism. In line with this optimistic outlook, research casts light on the possibilities and benefits of recategorization, so that people come to perceive a common group identity, and show less intergroup bias.[16] For example, when coworkers belonging to different ethnic groups see themselves as part of one common category, they express more coworker satisfaction.[17] The positive outcomes of common group identity probably arise through a revised perception of the (common) group, as constituting members who are more similar.[18]

The idea that a common-group identity leads to better group relationships builds on the pioneering research of Muzafer Sherif (1906–1988). Sherif's research demonstrated how intergroup competition and conflict can be transformed by the

---

[16] Gaertner et al. (1989).

[17] Cunningham (2005).

[18] Lemay and Ryan (2021).

members of different groups adopting *superordinate goals,* which are goals that all groups want to achieve, but no group can achieve without the cooperation of other groups.[19] The adoption of superordinate goals has become imperative, as all humanity is now confronted with the challenge of climate change and global warming. No nation can overcome global warming without the participation and cooperation of other nations. But we can make progress along an omnicultural path, because research points to possibilities for identifying with all of humanity, rather than just our own (ethnic, national, religious, or other) groups.

Ethnocentrism

As mentioned in Chaps. 1 and 6, ethnocentrism is a common human characteristic; most group members tend to see their group's way of life as natural and correct.[20] In addition, most group members show positive bias toward the ingroup, even when the differences between ingroup and outgroup are objectively trivial.[21] We tend to manufacture intergroup differences and magnify their importance in order to justify ethnocentrism and all kinds of biases in favor of our own group. However, there are exceptions, such as when minorities incorporate and act on negative stereotypes about themselves.

These exceptions are tragic, in the sense that they reveal how, as a result of experiencing severe discrimination and repression, some groups adopt negative and self-destructive stereotypes about themselves. However, these exceptions can teach us useful and important lessons, because they point to the malleability of human behavior in the domain of ethnocentrism. Thus, in order to learn the correct lessons from these exceptional cases, we need to pay close attention to them, as I discuss below.

In some cases, minorities tend to show a preference for the outgroup. Since the pioneering research of the African-American couple Kenneth (1914–2005) and Mamie Clark (1917–1983) from the 1940s, we have known that African-American children can incorporate negative stereotypes about their ethnic ingroup, and show a preference for white and other lighter colors. For example, when choosing between dolls of different colors, or when deciding on how to color images representing themselves, African-American children tended to choose white dolls and to color images representing themselves using colors that were lighter than their own skins.[22] These tendencies were detected in what became highly influential research by the

---

[19] Sherif (1966).

[20] Sumner (1906); LeVine and Campbell (1972); Balabanis and Siamagka (2022).

[21] Tajfel (1970).

[22] Clarck (1963) Clarck and Clarck (1950).

Clarks, indicating exceptions to the general tendency of group members to favor their own group.[23]

Research that illuminates how some minorities can adopt negative stereotypes about themselves and show bias against the ingroup and in favor of the outgroup demonstrates that ethnocentrism is malleable and can be reshaped. It is in the context of a racist culture and values that African-American children showed a preference for white dolls and lighter colors. Consequently, although ethnocentrism is generally seen as universal, or at least common among many (particularly majority) groups, social contexts can change this pattern. The malleability of ethnocentrism is also suggested by stereotype threat research, showing that the performance of women, ethnic minorities, and (even) White men in mathematics tests can be influenced (and reshaped) by the eliciting of threatening stereotypes that suggest their group should not do well in such tests (e.g., when White males take a mathematics test in a condition where they feel threatened by stereotypes of Asians being superior to Whites in quantitative skills).[24]

Thus, although research suggests that ethnocentrism is a common human characteristic, there is also strong evidence that context can (and does) change behavior in this area. Given the malleability of behavior in this domain, our challenge is to intentionally design contexts toward ending ethnocentrism—or at least limiting ethnocentrism in ways that result in less harm to outgroups, and to all society.

Self-Categorization, Recategorization, and Common-Group Identity

> The self-categorization analysis reconceptualizes the social group in predominantly cognitive terms as a 'collection of individuals who perceive themselves to be members of the same social category'…individuals who define, describe and evaluate themselves in terms of the social category and apply the ingroup's norms of conduct to themselves. The group is cognitively represented within the mind of the individual member and in this sense exists as a social identification.[25]

The above quotation is from a description of self-categorization theory, formulated by John Turner (1947–2011) and others, and reflects the dynamic, malleable, and changing nature of social categories—including important and commonly used social categories, such as "White" and "Black." Self-categorization theory focuses on how we categorize ourselves, with the understanding that such cognitive formulations of groups have the potential to change rapidly and dramatically, or to remain stable over long time periods. But even when we consider category boundaries as they operate in the larger society, the same flexibility and change can exist. For

---

[23] For the influence of research by the Clarcks, see Benjamin and Crouse (2004).

[24] Steele (2011) provides a highly insightful and reader-friendly account of this research, which he pioneered.

[25] Turner et al. (1987).

example, consider societies that have relied on so-called racial categories as central principles for their social, economic, and political organization. Even in these societies, the boundaries of categories such as "White" and "Black" are malleable and fuzzy. An example is Apartheid South Africa, where segregation was strictly based on so-called racial categories, but the interpretations of who belongs to each "racial category" and the criteria for deciding "racial category membership" were not stable—they changed over time, across regions of the country, and across organizations of the government agencies (such as the law courts versus the Department of Native Affairs in South Africa).[26]

The flexibility of social category boundaries suggests that groups are malleable and can be reconceptualized. Groups that were conceived as separate can be reformulated as one, and a group that is seen as one can be reformulated as multiple. This cognitive flexibility is already being used in training programs. For example, there are exercises available to help improve the cognitive flexibility of children in how they categorize the self, in order to achieve more positive emotions toward outgroups.[27] Children trained to work with multiple categorizations also show improvements in conceptual thinking, such as in proportional reasoning.[28] Thus, although categorization itself is a universal cognitive process, the boundaries and contents of categories are to some degree malleable and different across time and across societies.[29] The boundaries and contents of categories can be changed by design.

The malleability of social categories and the cognitive flexibility we humans have for categorizing the self and others mean that the groups we identify with and the groups we "celebrate as different" can change. This change can be designed to move in particular directions, including toward encompassing all humanity. As discussed in the next section, identifying with all humanity has enormously important benefits for all people.

Identifying with All Humanity

In this section I discuss research on identifying with all of humanity, and the benefits that arise from such identification. But identifying with all humanity also has risks, and I will also consider these. The psychologist who in modern times has contributed most extensively to our understanding of identifying with all humanity is Sam McFarland (1939–2022).[30] McFarland pointed out that although from ancient times there were exceptional individuals who expressed identification with all

---

[26] Posel (2001).

[27] Ray et al. (2008).

[28] Scheibling-Sève et al. (2022).

[29] See Keith (2013) and Moghaddam (2008, ch. 2).

[30] For example, see Hamer et al. (2019), McFarland (2011), McFarland et al. (2012), and McFarland et al. (2019).

humanity, such as Socrates about 2400 years ago and Tom Paine about 300 years ago, this sentiment has only recently become at least to some degree generally shared in the wider population. For example, when Portugal, Spain, France, England, and other Western colonial powers reached territories that were new to them in North and South America, Asia, and Africa, from the sixteenth to the nineteenth centuries, typically their attitude was that the local inhabitants did not have the rights of human beings, and they could be enslaved, owned, and treated as private property. The local inhabitants they found in these "newly discovered lands" (which were not at all new to the locals) were categorized outside the "human group." However, since at least the post-Second World War period, the idea that all human beings belong to the same group and have the same human rights has become more pervasively accepted throughout the world.

The ideal of identifying with all humanity is also reflected in, or at least raised by, the research of a number of influential modern psychologists, including Alfred Adler (1870–1937) and Gordon Allport (1897–1967). Adler conceived of humans as having a desire to help the larger human community, and Allport saw identification with humanity as a means of overcoming intergroup discrimination and conflict.[31] However, the most influential psychologist to directly address this issue is Abraham Maslow (1908–1970), particularly in his discussions of self-actualization as an ideal end in personality development. Maslow has argued that "Self-actualizing people have a deep feeling of identification, sympathy, and affection for human beings in general. They feel kinship and connection, as if all people were members of a single family…self-actualizing people have a genuine desire to help the human race."[32]

But Maslow also pointed to the enormous challenge of developing self-actualized individuals, and the difference between these individuals and everyone else, "Self-actualizing people are…very different from other people in thought, impulse, behavior, and emotion. When it comes down to it, in certain basic ways they are like aliens in a strange land."[33] Maslow's insight is important to keep in mind, as we discuss moving toward everyone achieving identification with all humanity. This is a long-term goal that will only be achieved through harnessing the power of education systems, as I discuss later in this section.

Since the early twentieth century, a number of research instruments have been developed to measure different aspects of identification with all humanity. These include measures of "internationalism," "worldmindedness," "Global Human Identity," "Human Identity Salience," "Cosmopolitan Orientation," and "Membership in the Global Human Community."[34] However, the most well-developed of such

---

[31] Adler (1927/1992); Allport (1954).

[32] Maslow (1970, p. 138).

[33] Maslow (1970, p. 138).

[34] These are reviewed by McFarland et al. (2019, pp. 145–148).

measures is the "Identification with All Humanity Scale," constructed by McFarland and colleagues.[35] A typical question on this scale is as follows:

Question: How close do you feel to each of the following groups?

(a) People in my community
(b) Americans
(c) All humans everywhere

Responses to these questions are typically registered in a continuous scale, from 1 ("not at all") to 5 ("very much"). In international research, the name of the country (subsection b) is changed from "Americans" to the name of the country in which the study is being carried out. Research using this measure in numerous countries has shown this to be a fairly reliable and valid measure with stable characteristics.[36] Through this research, we now have some solid ideas about the kind of people who identify with all humanity, as well as the correlates and possible consequences of identifying with all humanity.[37]

People who identify with all humanity tend to be more open to diversity and to new experiences, to be more empathic, and to see human beings and societies as interconnected.[38] In terms of correlates and possible consequences, research suggests that when people identify with all humanity, they become motivated to be less ethnocentric, to be more accepting toward outsiders, to cooperate with others to maximize collective outcomes, to be motivated to improve the lives of others, to adopt more pro-nature and pro-environment attitudes, and to act as more ethical consumers.[39] However, there is an important condition to the proposition that identifying with all humanity leads to these kinds of positive consequences. Research suggests that the consequences of identifying with all humanity are positive only when humans are thought to be benevolent (rather than malevolent).[40] In other words, if individuals believe humanity to be, for example, aggressive and cruel, their identification with humanity will probably result in harmful actions by them.

Another body of research that supports the idea that identifying with all humanity can have positive consequences arises from the common-group identity model.[41] The point of departure for this model is the extensive research literature on bias in favor of the ingroup, which we have already discussed in relation to ethnocentrism and the minimal group paradigm finding that even trivial differences between

---

[35] McFarland et al. (2012).

[36] Hamer et al. (2021).

[37] Of course, in this research it is safer to talk about the correlates, rather than the consequences, of identifying with all humanity. This is because "consequences" imply cause and effect, which is not always possible to identify.

[38] Hamer et al. (2019); McFarland et al. (2019), Reysen & Katzarska-Miller (2013).

[39] Ariely (2017), Buchan et al. (2011), Lee et al. (2015), Leung (2015), Nickerson & Louis (2008), Reysen et al. (2013), Reese and Kohlmann (2015). Also see Reysen and Katzarska-Miller (2012, 2013).

[40] Morton and Postmes (2011).

[41] Gaertner and Dovidio (2000).

groups can serve as a basis for ingroup bias (discussed in Chap. 4). Changing the cognitive representation of groups, so that all groups are now seen as part of the same "common ingroup," results in favoritism being shown toward everyone—because everyone is now a member of the same ingroup. An example would be if all people in the United States recategorize themselves as being part of the "American nation," instead of "immigrants versus Americans," and all people in Europe recategorize themselves as part of the group "Europeans," instead of "immigrants versus German, French, Italian…." Such recategorization from "us" versus "them" to "we" (encompassing everyone) has been empirically demonstrated to reduce intergroup prejudice, increase altruistic motives among majority group members, increase intergroup cooperation, and improve intergroup relations broadly.[42]

The common-group identity model also leads to a different interpretation of why improvements arise in intergroup relations, with reductions in prejudice and discrimination, as a result of greater contact between the members of different groups. This improvement could be because when the members of different groups have more contact with one another, they recategorize themselves as belonging to one common group.[43] According to this reinterpretation, intergroup contact has positive outcomes because of a shift in self-categorization.[44] That is, people move cognitively from "us" versus "them" to "we." This phenomenon was first empirically demonstrated by Muzafer Sherif, as discussed earlier in this chapter, through his research incorporating superordinate goals.

In important respects, the goals of common-group identity line up with the goals of assimilation policy. In both common-group identity and assimilation, the end result is assumed to be a unified group with a shared and common cognitive representation of "our group." However, as discussed in Chap. 4 in this text, assimilation policy is not designed to end group-based injustices in areas such as material resources. Rather, the focus is on cultural and linguistic assimilation, not an end to (even gross) injustices and group-based inequalities in material outcomes. Unfortunately, assimilation policy can be put into practice hand in hand with gigantic and unjust group-based inequalities.

This raises possible disadvantages to adopting a common-group identity, particularly from the perspective of minority groups. Most importantly, the adoption of a common-group identity could lessen the motivation of minority group members to agitate and collectively mobilize for progressive social change to end group-based inequalities, toward a more just society for all.[45] For example, in a society where minority groups suffer enormous economic and political disadvantages, the common-group identity feeling that "we are all one group" and "we are all in this together" could lessen the likelihood that disadvantaged group members will join movements to achieve change toward a more just society. However, a solution to

---

[42] Gaertner and Dovidio (2012), Kunst et al. (2015).

[43] Gaertner et al. (1996).

[44] This is in line with self-categorization theory (Turner et al., 1987).

[45] Saguy et al. (2009).

this possible shortcoming is to complement a primary focus on human commonalities with a secondary focus on group differences. This "dual identity" approach is in line with omniculturalism. Empirical evidence suggests that a dual identity, rather than a common-identity, approach leads to higher motivation for achieving social change toward a more just society.[46]

Educating the Omnicultural Global Citizen

The omnicultural citizen incorporates three components. The first component involves awareness and consciousness of global issues and the interconnected nature of the world. The second component consists of the personality characteristics that evolve to make the democratic citizen, capable of participating in and sustaining a democratic world. Finally, the third component involves the development of a global identity, central to which is identification as a global citizen inseparable from, and intricately connected with, the rest of humanity.

There has been some discussion of the kinds of education and training needed to teach young people about global issues and to make them aware of the interconnectedness of peoples and events in the world.[47] These discussions have led to a constructive exchange of ideas about the curriculum needs of schools and universities, intending to increase global awareness among students.[48] This research shows that we now have the basic educational methodology and curriculum content for educating young people to become more globally aware. Organizations such as OXFAM and UNESCO (United Nations Educational, Scientific and Cultural Organization) are contributing in important ways to this international discussion on education for global citizenship.[49]

An important insight from these discussions is that there are severe limits to the benefits of an education that highlights and celebrates group differences. As a representative of UNESCO explained, "The defense of authenticity is a human need, but it cannot seek to rupture the interdependence of humanity and the obvious necessity of 'living together'."[50] The same UNESCO representative adds, pointing to the limits of multicultural education, "Multi-cultural and multi-ethnic curricula have been used in societies that exploded, ripped apart by the forces that the education system bravely strove to tame."[51] This underlines the need for education to adopt an omnicultural approach and give highest priority to human commonalities, and only secondarily to intergroup differences.

---

[46] Glasford and Dovidio (2011).

[47] Hicks (2003), Ibrahim (2005), Pattiwael (2019), Smith et al. (2017).

[48] Blake et al. (2015); Dill (2013), Reysen et al. (2013).

[49] OXFAM (n.d.-a, n.d.-b).

[50] Pigozzi (2006, p. 1).

[51] Pigozzi (2006, p. 2).

The second key feature of the omnicultural citizen consists of the personality characteristics that help bring to life the democratic citizen. This component is essential and integral to developing democracy. The democratic citizen is capable of participating in and sustaining an actualized or "fully developed" democratic society, both at local and global levels.[52] The ten minimal personality characteristics of the democratic citizen are discussed below. What I am presenting here is an ideal, in the utopian tradition of Thomas More (1478–1535) and others.[53] I believe such ideals are invaluable in lifelong education of collectives and individuals, because they help to inspire and guide action—even though we might never reach the pure ideal that is espoused.

1. *I could be wrong.*
   For the democratic citizen, the point of departure in any social, cultural, or political interaction and exchange with others is the starting acknowledgement that "I could be wrong." This seemingly simple step is actually extremely difficult to achieve, particularly for individuals who are low on tolerance for ambiguity, and high on categorical thinking and dogmatism. For example, religious and political fundamentalists find it extremely difficult to acknowledge "I could be wrong." This is because they begin interactions on the assumption that "I am right, and anyone who disagrees with me is wrong." Thus, the first step in education toward socializing the omnicultural citizen is to nurture within individuals the capability to acknowledge "I could be wrong." This capability opens the door to possibilities for change and growth, at both individual and collective levels.

2. *I must critically question everything, including the sacred beliefs of my society.*
   Beyond individuals critically self-reflecting and thinking hard about the possibility that "I could be wrong," they must also develop the capability to question even the sacred beliefs of their own societies. Every society holds certain beliefs and assumptions that are treated as sacred and that individuals within each society are socialized to incorporate within their own identities and accept as valid. We very seldom question such societal beliefs and assumptions, which are associated with ethnocentrism, nationalism, and racial and cultural stereotypes that underlie conceptions of the special (and generally superior) characteristics of "our people." Almost a century of psychological research on conformity and obedience informs us that most of us conform and obey according to what we understand to be "correct" behavior in our society, even when we are aware that the beliefs and assumptions in our societies are incorrect, and even when our conformity and obedience can harm others.[54] Consequently, it is imperative that from a young age, children are socialized to have the capacity to question even

---

[52] These personality characteristics and the concept of actualized democracy were first discussed in detail in Moghaddam (2016).

[53] More (2005/1516).

[54] The psychological research on conformity and obedience is reviewed in Moghaddam (2005), chapters 15 and 16.

the sacred beliefs of their own societies. This questioning is integral to the wider capacity to develop critical thinking.

3. *I must revise my opinions as the evidence requires.*

Our opinions are influenced by the evidence we know about and accept as valid. At any one time, we are aware of only a small part of all the possible evidence. Some of this evidence is stable, but much of it is uncertain and changes over time. For example, our opinions about what led to a particular war between two nations, or what kinds of vaccines are necessary for children, or how much and what kinds of foods we should eat to remain healthy, are influenced by information that tends to change over time. But in order to benefit from the new evidence that comes to light, individuals must be flexible and open to reviewing and incorporating the new evidence—and changing their opinions if the evidence requires such change.

Of course, this process is not just a matter of individual decision-making and change. Each individual functions within social networks, and the opinions of individuals are upheld not only by themselves as isolated individuals but also by the social scaffolding surrounding them. This social scaffolding consists of all the individuals and groups, as well as the larger cultural system, which influence the individual. If the scaffolding is rigid and unchanging, then individuals have to struggle very hard to change their personal opinions. In essence, individuals must be socialized to have the capacity to act as nonconformists and to be disobedient, when this is required of them in order to revise their opinions in line with new evidence.

4. *I must seek to understand those who are different from me.*

Human beings tend to seek closer interactions and relationships with others who are similar to them, rather than different from them (a topic we discussed in Chap. 3). Our tendency is to keep our distance from people who are different from us. But this behavioral tendency means that we miss many invaluable opportunities to better understand others who are different from us, and to also learn important lessons from them. But the current cultural traditions of most societies are to socialize young people to steer clear of others who are different. An integral part of omnicultural education is to change this tendency, so that instead of avoiding those who are different from us, we are more open to getting to know and better understand them.

5. *I must learn from those who are different from me.*

Those who are different from us represent rich possibilities for us to broaden our horizons and improve ourselves as individuals and groups. Of course, we can also learn valuable lessons from those who are similar to us. For example, elders who are part of our ingroup can teach us invaluable lessons about the cultural practices and traditions of our ingroup. However, those who are different from us can present us with opportunities to learn about alternative ways of perceiving and interacting with the world, as well as new ways of identifying, interpreting, and solving problems. But in order to take advantage of these opportunities, we must adopt an open-minded perspective toward those who are different from us, and come to appreciate that we can learn from them and in this way improve ourselves.

6. *I must seek information and opinions from different sources.*

The rapid increase in information and opinion sources influenced by electronic communications and artificial intelligence (AI) has created rapidly expanding opportunities for people to become better informed, but also brought grave new dangers associated with fake news and misinformation. Research shows that problems associated with the spreading of fake news and misinformation generally arise when people do not have the necessary relevant knowledge and fail to apply careful reasoning.[55] This points to a great need to start training at an early age on how information should be gathered, critically assessed, and used. We need to educate children to seek information and opinions from a wide variety of sources, and to critically evaluate what they find. It has become absolutely essential that this kind of critical thinking is taught from the earliest years of schooling, as there is increased influence of AI and electronic communications on almost all of the information we receive, including when we are children.[56]

7. *I should be actively open to new experiences.*

Groups and individuals who are different from us can provide us with experiences that are in significant ways enriching and rewarding. These are the kinds of experiences that we are not able to find within our own groups. But in order to benefit from such experiences, we need to be open to interacting with others who are different from us and participating in the experiences they offer us. This kind of openness needs to be nurtured in people through appropriate education from an early age. Some individuals will already be high on the personality trait "openness to experience" and be more ready to take advantage of opportunities to learn from experiences offered by others, but many individuals will be low on openness to experience and will need additional educational training to acquire this benefit.[57]

8. *I should be open to creating new experiences for others.*

Being open to creating new experiences for others is the other side of the coin to oneself being actively open to new experiences that are created by others. The benefits of creating new experiences for others do not only accrue to the individuals who have the new experience, but also to those individuals who provide the new experience. For example, when Jill and Jack guide two Chinese visitors through the details of an American Thanksgiving Day, they also get an opportunity to reflect back on the meaning of Thanksgiving for Americans. In the process of responding to questions from the Chinese visitors, Jill and Jack

---

[55] Pennycook and Rand (2021).

[56] Wang et al. (2022).

[57] Individual differences on openness to experience are associated with creativity and intellect (Kaufman et al., 2016). Openness to experience is no doubt influenced by both genetic and environmental factors and (following epigenetic research) can be influenced through experiential interventions.

come to see Thanksgiving from new angles and appreciate their own traditions in new ways.

9. *There are principles of right and wrong.*

The first eight characteristics of the democratic citizen listed above could lead to a serious danger, that of pursuing a relativist path that denies any absolute principles of right and wrong. From this relativist stand, the merit of all judgements is relative to the perspective of observers and their cultures (this is a topic we initially discussed in Chap. 1). For example, from a relativist perspective, the treatment of women in Iran (under the rule of the mullahs), Afghanistan (under the rule of the Taliban), and similar dictatorships controlled by Islamic fundamentalists cannot be judged as unjust, because there are no universal principles of right and wrong in how women and men should be treated, and each society has the right to treat people according to its own internal laws. In rejecting this position, I believe we can and must develop and apply universal principles of right and wrong that benefit all humankind.[58] However, we must take great care that the universal principles adopted, which will be few, truly reflect the interests and priorities of all humanity, and not just those who enjoy greater power, not just the high-income countries, and not just the richest groups within these countries.

10. *I should actively seek experiences of higher value.*

Just as there are universal principles of right and wrong, some experiences have higher value than other experiences. Individuals should be educated to seek experiences of higher value. Again, judgements about the value of different experiences must be made with the interests and priorities of all humankind in mind. The focus will remain on what all humans have on common, and the values and norms that are shared by everyone. These values and norms will be few, but they must be given highest priority.

Concluding Comment

Empirical evidence suggests that omniculturalism can lead to valuable improvements in human social relations. By giving highest priority to the many important ways in which we humans are similar, to what we have in common, we can recategorize everyone as part of the ingroup. Consequently, the bias we typically show in favor of the ingroup now accrues to all humans. At a secondary level, we acknowledge that there are also some differences between people, and this leaves room for a need for distinctiveness. However, the highest priority remains on the most inclusive category—"we humans."

---

[58] Geertz (1984) puts forward a set of arguments against anti-relativism, but does not address the moral need for universal principles in areas such as human rights.

Of course, it could be argued that the "ingroup" should be even broader and should include all living creatures, and all of nature (including all animals and plants). This is a compelling argument. However, as we discussed, research shows that people who identify with all humanity also have more positive relationships with nature and the physical environment. Thus, by implication, if we arrive at a position where all humanity is included in our ingroup, we will also improve our relationship with nature. Related to this, omnicultural individuals are not only more pro-nature; they also have more of the characteristics of the democratic citizen, capable of actively participating in and supporting democracy.

The ideal of omniculturalism and that of the democratic citizen can only be achieved through appropriate education programs. The core of such programs has already been explored in association with identifying with all humanity and, at least since the time of John Dewey (1859–1852), educating citizens for democracy. We have the basic knowledge about the kind of education that will result in individuals capable of participating in and helping to implement omniculturalism. We need to make changes in our ideologies and policies, from manufacturing, highlighting, and celebrating differences between people (including fictional and surface differences) to giving highest priority to the many foundational ways in which all humans are similar to one another.

References

Adler, A. (1992). *Understanding human nature* (C. Brett, Trans.). Hazelden. (Original work published 1927).

Allport, G. W. (1954). *The nature of prejudice*. Addison-Wesley.

Ariely, G. (2017). Global identification, xenophobia and globalization: A cross-national exploration. *International Journal of Psychology, 52*, 87–96.

Ashe, A., Colot, V., & Oldroyd, B. P. (2021). How does epigenetics influence the course of evolution? *Philosophical Transactions of the Royal Society B, 376*, 20200111. https://doi.org/10.1098/rstb.2020.0111

Berry, J. A., Ebner, D., & Cornelius, M. (2019). White identity politics: Linked fate and political participation. *Politics, Groups and Identities*. https://doi.org/10.1080/21565503.2019.1615965

Balabanis, G., & Siamagka, N. T. (2022). A meta-analysis of consumer ethnocentrism across 57 countries. *International Journal of Research in Marketing, 39*, 745–763.

Benjamin, L. T., & Crouse, E. M. (2004). The American Psychological Association's response to Brown v. Board of Education: The case of Kenneth B. Clark. *American Psychologist, 57*, 38–50.

Blake, M. E., Pierce, L., Gibson, S., Reysen, S., & Katzarska-Miller, I. (2015). University environment and global citizenship identification. *Journal of Educational and Developmental Psychology, 5*, 97–107.

Buchan, N. R., Brewer, M. B., Grimalda, G., Wilson, R. K., Fatas, E., & Foddy, M. (2011). Global social identity and global cooperation. *Psychological Science, 22*, 821–828.

Clarck, K. B. (1963). *Prejudice and your child*. Beacon Press.

Clarck, K. B., & Clarck, M. P. (1950). Emotional factors in racial identification and preference in negro children. *The Journal of Negro Education, 19*, 341–350.

Cunningham, G. B. (2005). The importance of common in-group identity in ethnically diverse groups. *Group Dynamics: Theory, Research, and Practice, 9*, 251–260.

Dill, J. D. (2013). *The longings and limits of global citizenship education: The moral pedagogy of schooling in a cosmopolitan age*. Routledge.

Gaertner, S. L., & Dovidio, J. F. (2000). *Reducing intergroup bias: The common group identity model*. Psychology Press.

Gaertner, S. L., & Dovidio, J. F. (2012). Reducing intergroup bias: The common ingroup identity model. In P. A. M. Van Lange, A. W. Kruglanski, & E. T. Higgins (Eds.), *Handbook of theories of social psychology* (Vol. 2, pp. 439–457). Sage.

Gaertner, S. L., Dovidio, J. F., & Bachman, B. A. (1996). Revisiting the contact hypothesis: The induction of a common group identity. *International Journal of Intercultural Relations, 20*, 271–290.

Gaertner, S. L., Mann, J., Murrell, A., & Dovidio, J. F. (1989). Reducing intergroup bias: The benefits of recategorization. *Journal of Personality and Social Psychology, 57*, 239–249.

Geertz, C. (1984). Anti anti-relativism. *American Anthropologist, 86*, 263–278.

Glasford, D. E., & Dovidio, J. F. (2011). E pluribus unum: Dual identity and minority group members' motivation to engage in contact, as well as social change. *Journal of Experimental Social Psychology, 47*, 1021–1024.

Gould, S. J. (1996). *The mismeasure of man*. Norton.

Hamer, K., McFarland, S., & Penczek, M. (2019). What lies beneath? Predictors of identification with all humanity. *Personality and Individual Differences, 141*, 258–267.

Hamer, K., Penczek, M., McFarland, S., Wlodarczyk, A., Luzniak-Piecha, M., Golinska, A., Cadena, L. M., Ibarra, M., Bertin, P., & Delouvee, S. (2021). Identification with all humanity—A test of the factorial structure and measurement invariance of the scale in five countries. *International Journal of Psychology, 56*, 157–174.

Hicks, D. (2003). Thirty years of global education: A reminder of key principles and precedents. *Educational Review, 55*, 265–275.

Ibrahim, T. (2005). Global citizenship education: Mainstreaming the curriculum? *Cambridge Journal of Education, 35*, 177–194.

Kant, E. (2002). Groundwork for the metaphysics of morals. In A. W. Wood (Ed. & Trans.). Yale University Press. (Original work published 1785).

Kaufman, S. B., Quilty, L. C., Grazioplene, R. G., Hirsh, J. B., Gray, J. R., Peterson, J. B., & DeYoung, C. G. (2016). Openness to experience and intellect differentially predict creative achievement in the arts and sciences. *Journal of Personality, 84*(2), 248–258.

Keith, K. D. (2013). Categorization. In K. D. Keith (Ed.), *The encyclopedia of cross-cultural psychology* (Vol. 1, pp. 160–161). Wiley-Blackwell.

Kunst, J. R., Thomsen, L., Sam, D. L., & Berry, J. W. (2015). "We are in this together": Common group identity predicts majority members' active acculturation efforts to integrate immigrants. *Personality and Social Psychology Bulletin, 4*, 1438–1453.

Lee, K., Ashton, M. C., Choi, J., & Zachariassen, K. (2015). Connectedness to nature and to humanity: Their association and personality correlates. *Frontiers in Psychology, 6*. https://doi.org/10.3389/fpsyg.2015.01003

Lee, N., Lessem, E., & Moghaddam, F. M. (2008). Standing out and blending in: Differentiation and conflict. In F. M. Moghaddam, R. Harré, & N. Lee (Eds.), *Global conflict resolution through positioning analysis* (pp. 113–131). Springer.

Lemay, E. P., & Ryan, J. E. (2021). Common group identity, perceived similarity, and communal interracial relationships. *Personality and Social Psychology Bulletin, 47*, 985–1003.

Lerner, M. (1980). *The belief in a just world: A fundamental delusion*. Plenum Press.

Leung, A. K. Y., Koh, K., & Tam, K. P. (2015). Being environmentally responsible: Cosmopolitan orientation predicts pro-environmental behaviors. *Journal of Environmental Psychology, 43*, 79–94.

LeVine, R. A., & Campbell, D. T. (1972). *Ethnocentrism: Theories of conflict, ethnic attitudes, and group behavior*. Wiley.

Maslow, A. (1970). *Motivation and personality* (3rd ed.). Harper & Row.

McFarland, S. (2011). The slow creation of humanity. *Political Psychology, 32*, 1–20.

McFarland, S., Hackett, J., Hamer, K., Katzarska-Miller, I., Malsch, A., Reese, G., & Reysen, S. (2019). Global human identification and citizenship: A review of psychological studies. *Advances in Political Psychology, 40*, 141–171.

McFarland, S., Webb, M., & Brown, D. (2012). All humanity is my ingroup: A measure and studies of "Identification with all humanity". *Journal of Personality and Social Psychology, 103*, 830–851.

Moghaddam, F. M. (2005). Great ideas in psychology. *Oneworld*.

Moghaddam, F. M. (2008). *Multiculturalism and intergroup relations: Implications for democracy in global context*. American Psychological Association Press.

Moghaddam, F. M. (2009). Omniculturalism: Policy solutions to fundamentalism in the era of fractured globalization. *Culture & Psychology, 15*, 337–347.

Moghaddam, F. M. (2012). The omnicultural imperative. *Culture & Psychology, 18*, 304–330.

Moghaddam, F. M. (2016). *The psychology of democracy*. American Psychological Association.

Moghaddam, F. M. (2023a). *How psychologists failed: We neglected the poor and minorities, favored the rich and privileged, and got science wrong*. Cambridge University Press.

Moghaddam, F. M. (2023b). *Political plasticity: The future of democracy and dictatorship*. Cambridge University Press.

More, T. (2005). *Utopia* (Trans. R. Robinson). Barnes & Noble. Originally published in 1516.

Morton, T. A., & Postmes, T. (2011). What does it mean to be human? How salience of human category affects responses to intergroup harm. *European Journal of Social Psychology, 41*, 866–873.

Nickerson, A. M., & Louis, W. R. (2008). Nationality versus humanity? Personality, identity, and norms in relation to attitudes toward asylum seekers. *Journal of Applied Social Psychology, 38*, 796–817.

O'Neill, O. (1989). *Constructions of reason: Explorations of Kant's practical philosophy*. Cambridge University Press.

OXFAM. (n.d.-a). *Education for global citizenship: A guide for schools*. https://oxfamilibrary. openrepository.com/bitstream/handle/10546/620105/edu-global-citizenship-schools-guide-091115-en.pdf?sequence=11&isAllowed=y

OXFAM. (n.d.-b). *What is global citizenship?* https://www.oxfam.org.uk/education/who-we-are/what-is-global-citizenship/. Accessed April 3, 2024.

Pattiwael, A. S. (2019). Literature for developing students' humanity awareness. *Journal International Seminar on Languages, Literature, Art and Education (ISLLAE), 1*, 79–88.

Pennycook, G., & Rand, D. G. (2021). The psychology of fake news. *Trends in Cognitive Sciences, 25*, 388–402.

Pigozzi, M. J. (2006). A UNESCO view of global citizenship education. *Educational Review, 58*, 1–4.

Plato. (1987). *The Republic* (D. Lee, Trans.). Penguin.

Plaut, V. C., Thomas, K. M., Hurd, K., & Romano, C. A. (2018). Do colorblindness and multiculturalism remedy or foster discrimination and racism? *Current Directions in Psychological Science, 27*, 200–206.

Posel, D. (2001). Race as common sense: Racial classification in twentieth-century South Africa. *African Studies Review, 44*, 87–113.

Rawls, J. (1971). *A theory of justice*. Belknap Press of Harvard University Press.

Ray, D. G., Mackie, D. M., Rydell, R. J., & Smith, E. R. (2008). Changing categorization of self can change emotions about outgroups. *Journal of Experimental Social Psychology, 44*, 1210–1213.

Reese, G., & Kohlmann, F. (2015). Feeling global, acting ethically: Global identification and fairtrade consumption. *The Journal of Social Psychology, 155*, 98–106.

Reysen, S., & Katzarska-Miller, I. (2012). College course curriculum and global citizenship. *International Journal of Developmental Education and Global Learning, 4*, 27–39.

Reysen, S., & Katzarska-Miller, I. (2013). A model of global citizenship: Antecedents and outcomes. *International Journal of Psychology, 48*, 858–870.

Reysen, S., Pierce, L., & Spencer, C. J. (2013). Exploring the content of global citizen identity. *The Journal of Multiculturalism in Education, 9*, 1–31.

Saguy, T., Tausch, N., Dovidio, J. F., & Pratto, F. (2009). The irony of harmony: Intergroup contact can produce false expectations for equality. *Psychological Science, 20*, 114–121.

Scheibling-Sève, C., Gvozdic, K., Pasquinelli, E., & Sander, E. (2022). Enhancing cognitive flexibility through a training based on multiple categorization: Developing proportional reasoning in primary school. *Journal of Numerical Cognition, 8*, 443–472.

Sherif, M. (1966). *Group conflict and cooperation: Their social psychology*. Routledge & Kegan Paul.

Smith, W. C., Fraser, P., Chykina, V., Ikoma, S., Levitan, J., Liu, J., & Mahfouz, J. (2017). Global citizenship and the importance of education in a globally integrated world. *Globalisation, Societies and Education, 15*, 648–665.

Steele, C. (2011). *Whistling Vivaldi: How stereotypes affect us and what we can do*. W.W. Norton.

Sumner, W. G. (1906). *Folkways*. Ginn.

Tajfel, H. (1970). Experiments in intergroup discrimination. *Scientific American, 223*, 96–108.

Tajfel, H., & Turner, J. C. (1979). An integrative theory of intergroup conflict. In W. G. Austin & S. Worchel (Eds.), *The social psychology of intergroup relations* (pp. 33–47). Brooks/Cole.

Turner, J. C., Hogg, M. A., Oakes, P. J., Reicher, S. D., & Wetherell, M. S. (1987). *Rediscovering the social group: A self-categorization theory*. Basil Blackwell.

Wang, G., Zhao, J., Van Kleek, M., & Shadbolt, N. (2022). Informing age-appropriate AI: Examining principles and practices of ai for children. In *Proceedings of the 2022 CHI conference on human factors in computing systems* (pp. 1–29). https://doi.org/10.1145/3491102.3502057

Whitley, B. E., Littrell, A., & Schultz, T. (2023). The measurement of racial colorblindness. *Personality and Social Psychology Bulletin, 49*, 1531–1351.

Chapter 8
Our Omnicultural World

Human beings are members of a whole,
In creation of one essence and soul.

This verse celebrating the unity of humankind by the Persian poet Sa'adi (c. 1213–1291) is very well known; it adorns the entrance to the Hall of Nations in the United Nations Building in New York, and has been quoted numerous times by celebrities.[1] The theme of human unity and commonality is widely celebrated in art, which is often described as a universal language.[2] The greatest creative thinkers working in many different languages have in numerous ways reflected on the universal nature of the most important human characteristics. Here is Shylock, in Shakespeare's (1564–1616) play *The Merchant of Venice*, elaborating on human similarities

:...I am a Jew.
Hath not a Jew eyes? Hath not a Jew hands, organs,
dimensions, senses, affections, passions, fed with
the same food, hurt with the same weapons, subject
to the same diseases, heal'd by the same means,
warm'd and cool'd by the same winter and summer,
as a Christian is? If you prick us, do we not bleed?
If you tickle us, do we not laugh? If you
poison us, do we not die? (III.i.58–66)[3]

---

[1] President Barack Obama quoted Sa'adi in his message to Iranians in March 2009. The British rock band Coldplay used the title "Bani Adam" in their album "Everyday Life" (released 2019) with reference to "Saadi Shirazi" (track number 6 under "Sunset").

[2] Brinkmann et al. (2014) present evidence to suggest that the argument for art being a universal language does not stretch to abstract art.

[3] *The Riverside Shakespeare: The complete works.* 2nd. Ed 1997.

Shakespeare was writing at a time when colonization of distant territories in Africa, Asia, and the Americas was for the first time bringing Western explorers into direct contact with non-Western peoples. The relationship between colonizers and indigenous peoples is a central theme in Shakespeare's plays. A prime example is the relationship between Prospero, the foreign and all-powerful "colonizer" who arrived in the new land with his daughter Miranda, and Caliban, the relatively powerless native, in the play *Othello*. During their sometimes extraordinarily difficult journeys to distant lands, Western travelers recognized that nature treats all humans in the same way, irrespective of their worldly rank, title, and wealth. This becomes clear at the start of Shakespeare's play *The Tempest*, when the king and his royal entourage are on board a ship caught in a gigantic storm, and one of the courtiers reminds a sailor that the king is onboard. The sailor's response is, "What cares these/roarers for the name of the king?" (I.i.16–17).[4] The sailor is certain that nature treats kings and all other human beings in the same way.

Kant also would have human beings treat one another in the same manner, as an end in itself, and not as a means to an end. This arises from Kant's categorical imperative that we discussed in Chap. 7, which has implications for how we should treat both others and ourselves.[5] An implication for the self is that we have a duty to maintain a healthy level of self-respect, and not to degrade ourselves. We must not be servile, fawning, and groveling in our relationships with others, no matter how much more powerful and wealthy they are than us. One's status as a human being is equal to all other human beings and it is constant, independent of one's fortune, status, and power. Each of us has worth and dignity simply because of our status as a human being.

According to Kant, just as our duty to ourselves means that we must maintain a healthy level of self-respect, our duty to others means that we must respect all other human beings. This respect is not dependent on the rank, wealth, power, talents, moral standing, or achievements of others. Rather, respect for other human beings is unconditional; it is demanded by their human standing. Thus, just as the storm in Shakespeare's play *The Tempest* treats the king, the courters, and the sailors in exactly the same way, we must treat all other humans with the same level of high respect.

Of course, Kant is using the categorical imperative to set up an ideal to which he wants us to aspire. In practice, we are far from this idea. Although nature cares not who is a royal king and who is a mere sailor, and treats everyone the same, human beings themselves treat each other very differently, depending on their category memberships (wealth, ethnicity, and so on). Indeed, rather than treat all humans as members of the same human group, the current tendency is to look for, to highlight, and to celebrate differences between human groups, even fabricated ones. A challenge taken up by omniculturalism is to focus on and celebrate human commonalities, to recognize how we are in the most important ways similar to one another.

---

[4] Folger Shakespeare Library, *The Tempest*, 1994.

[5] Kant (2002).

Each and every one of us merits equal and unconditional respect as human beings. Omniculturalism acknowledges our differences, but treats them as being of secondary importance.

In Part I of this chapter, I examine the ways in which major religions, political ideologies, and utopian thinkers have attempted to achieve human unity. The main focus of these efforts has been on the ways in which other humans, all those who are not part of our ingroup, will need to change in order for us to achieve human unity. The idea is that they, all those other humans, must change to become like us, so they can be accepted as one of us. In Part II, I explain that in contrast to this "conquering" approach to uniting humanity, omniculturalism proposes that the ground is prepared for our unity because on an objective basis all human beings *already are* very similar in the most important ways. The change that needs to take place is for subjective attention and priority to be given to human commonalities that already objectively exist, rather than to human differences. I argue that one way to give more attention to, and to prioritize, human similarities, is to attend more to common themes in world art and literature. This is of special importance in the socialization of the young.

Traditional Paths to Human Unity: Conquering Others

The ideal of human unity, getting to "one world," is shared by the major religions of the world, including Judaism, Christianity, and Islam. Each of these religions envisages an ideal world in which all humanity recognizes "the truth" and adopts the beliefs of *the* one true religion. Of course, the followers of every religion believe that they alone represent the one true religion; only they see the truth. According to the traditional religions, the end goal of one humanity would be achieved by everyone accepting the truth according to this particular faith, and abandoning the alternative "false" paths. Historically, this kind of conversion to accept a particular truth represented by one of the major religions has been achieved through military and/or economic conquest. Those faithful to a particular religion would conquer land and/or become economically and politically dominant in a region, drive out those who refuse to convert to their religion, and absorb those who become believers and one of the privileged ingroup "who will be saved." This tragic process has repeatedly taken place in the Middle East in the early twenty-first century.

Fierce competition, and sometimes violent conflict, between followers of different religions tends to obscure the idealized end goal shared by the faithful of the different major religions. They all believe that the world will become united and peaceful when everyone else converts and accepts "our truth." Of course, because each group of faithful followers is strongly tied (economically, politically, culturally, emotionally) to their own religion, there is fierce inter-religious competition and violent conflicts. No group of religious believers are ready to abandon their own group and convert to another religion without a fight. Also, there are strict punishments, ranging from ostracism to death depending on the religious group and the circumstances, for those who abandon the religion into which they were born.

Consequently, although there are some changes in the size and vigor of the different religious groups, there is also a lot of stability, at least in the short term.[6]

The idea of reaching one world and one humanity through conquest is also common to political ideologies of both the political left and the political right, which in this respect are very similar to religious movements. For example, communists repeatedly appeal to the "workers of the world" and envisage reaching the ideal one world through class warfare and revolution at the global level.[7] They believe that the proletariat revolution against capitalism, followed by the dictatorship of the proletariat, will eventually lead to a classless society across the world. At this final stage, the world will be united and free of oppression. There will be no centralized governments, because such governments only function to protect the interests of the ruling class, and when there is no capitalist ruling class, then there is no need for governments. This idealized communist world is envisaged as one humanity, one world in peace.

But the idealized "one world" envisaged by communists is arrived at through conquest, just as surely as the major religions have tried to arrive at their version of one world, with everyone converting to their particular faith, through conquest. The terms "class warfare" and "class conflict" are used by communists in a literal as well as a metaphorical sense. The revolutions that brought communists to power in Russia (1917), China (1949), and Cuba (1959) were as violent as revolutions that brought to power religious groups in modern times, such as the ones in Iran (where the mullahs established a religious dictatorship in 1979) and in Afghanistan (where the Taliban returned to dictatorial power in 2021). This similarity extends to revolutionaries of the political right. For example, the Nazis in Germany and the fascists in Italy both used brute force to grab power in the first half of the twentieth century, and they intended to conquer the rest of the world to bring about their Nazi/fascist version of one world. It took the Second World War (1939–1945) to stop them.

Thus, the idea of "one world," "one humanity," and "human unity" has been pursued through conquest by a wide variety of religious and political movements, at least over the last few thousand years or so. The basic idea has been the same for all these movements: that everybody else on earth should convert to our religion/ideology (which is the only correct one) and, in this way, we shall arrive at a united and peaceful world. This will represent the end of history, such as the communist ideal of one classless society across all the world. Another version of the end of history thesis arose from the political right, after the collapse of the Soviet Union in 1990. This was when political right-wing pundits in the United States predicted that communism had been conquered and the end of history would involve all the different societies in the world turning into capitalist democracies.[8] Events proved them wrong. Capitalist democracies did not blossom. Instead, in the twenty-first century,

---

[6] Johnson and Grim (2013).

[7] Marx and Engels (2021/1848).

[8] Fukuyama (1992).

we have witnessed the weakening of democracies, the strengthening of dictatorships, and the rise of authoritarian strongmen, including in the United States.[9]

Rather than achieving one world and one humanity through conquest, omniculturalism proposes that *we already have* one humanity in the sense that all human beings are very similar in foundational characteristics. These common human characteristics are to a large extent already identified by scientific research, such as research in the biological and psychological sciences.[10] The challenge is, first, to recognize, to highlight, give priority to, and celebrate human commonalities and, second, to also acknowledge human differences, but as being of secondary importance.

The Omnicultural Path to World Unity

> Historical universalism sees the history of all humankind as a unity…Political universalism sees all humankind as one political entity, to be governed under a world state and a benevolent world government. Religious universalism sees all religions as unified on the basis of a common experience known to all mystics in all ages and cultures: the experience of the Light…Philosophical universalism focuses on the universe as did the great philosophers of the past.[11]

In order to make progress, then, omniculturalism requires that changes come about in our psychological outlook. We must shift from looking for differences, manufacturing differences, and celebrating differences to recognizing and celebrating human commonalities. The first step, in line with Kant, is unconditional respect for oneself and respect for others because of our membership in the human group. The second step is to recognize that all humans are very similar in foundational ways, but also different in less important ways. Every child in every society should be taught that we humans are far more similar than we are different.

Thus, omniculturalism points to and builds upon the theme of universalism, which Nicholas Haggar (quoted above) argues is already present in various important domains, including in history, religion, philosophy, and of course literature—a domain that Haggar himself explores, with a focus on the fundamental theme and unity of world literature. The interconnected nature and unity of world literature can be explored by identifying common themes. Of course, what are claimed to be universal themes are sometimes contested. For example, consider Robert McKee's claim that there is a classical design to world literature, and Joseph Campbell's argument that an example of a universal quest theme is the hero's journey, the

---

[9] Moghaddam (2019).

[10] The discovery of universals is the explicit goal of biological and psychological sciences, as reflected even in introductory courses to these disciplines. For example, see Johnson (2016) for biology and Kalat (2022) for psychology.

[11] Haggar (2012, pp. 1–2).

protagonist overcoming obstacles on the road to reach a goal.[12] The hero's journey as a universal theme has been criticized, as an example of how individualistic Western values are projected onto non-Western literature.[13] However, I believe some such criticisms are misleading, a point I clarify below by discussing the distinction between two types of commonalities.

To what extent is a characteristic common only to a specific society or a few societies, and to what extent is a characteristic common to most or even all societies? The terms emics and etics have come to refer to these two types of commonalities, with emics representing the characteristics of one or a few societies and etics representing the characteristics of most or all societies.[14] An important point is that to qualify as an etic, a characteristic does not have to be shared by all human societies but only by most of them. Thus, when critics point to one or a few exceptions to a general rule, such exceptions do not bring the entire edifice crashing down and negate the possibility of a characteristic representing an etic—as long as we can show that a characteristic is shared by most human societies (or most human individuals, when we are dealing with individual characteristics).

With respect to the kinds of evidence we can put forward to demonstrate the existence of etics, I have already referred to empirical research in domains such as psychological science which, as traditionally conceived, involves the scientific discovery of universals in human behavior. Particularly in domains such as biological psychology, sensation, perception, learning, cognition, memory, emotions, and motivation, even basic introductory psychology texts discuss behaviors that qualify as etics, that is, behaviors that are common to most and sometimes all people. For example, categorization is an etic feature of cognition.[15] The contents of categories can vary across cultures, but all humans (and many animals) engage in the cognitive act of categorization. There are also other extremely important types of evidence that are often overlooked, and these concern world literatures both across time within cultures and also within time across cultures.

Let us first consider how we read and enjoy literature across time within cultures. I was born in Iran and my mother tongue is Farsi, the official language of Iran, but also used by some people in other countries in the region (e.g., Afghanistan, Tajikistan). There is an extraordinarily rich literary tradition in Farsi, with truly great poetry going back thousands of years. One reason for the depth and vitality of Farsi poetry is that all kinds of Farsi-speaking scientists, philosophers, and thinkers used poetry, rather than prose, to express themselves. Historically, Farsi speakers have not produced novels, essays, or other works of prose at a high level, but they have produced world-class poetry.

---

[12] McKee and El-Wakil (2022); Campbell (2003).

[13] See Campbell (2003) and Hambly (2021).

[14] Engler and Whitesides (2022) provide an example of how emic characteristics can serve to build up a picture of etics in the domain of religion.

[15] Harnad (2017).

Another very special feature of Farsi poetry, including the classical works of Ferdowsi (940–1020), Rumi (1207–1273), Sa'adi (c. 1213–1291), and Hafez (c. 1325–1390), is that they are very widely known and recited among Farsi speakers—including illiterate individuals. Farsi-speaking people have a very strong oral tradition; a great deal of their traditional knowledge, values, mythologies, and cultural worldview are passed on orally from generation to generation.[16] As a child in Tehran, I was amazed at the enormous numbers of lines of poetry even illiterate workers could recite by heart. Of course, I faced the challenge of memorizing Farsi poetry to recite in my school classes, but many of the manual laborers who did their work while singing and reciting poetry all day had never attended school. Some of them could recite thousands of lines of classical verse, and they could debate a topic by selecting appropriate verses from memory.

How is it that these "illiterate" workers could recite classical Farsi poetry from a thousand years ago, and see this poetry as directly applicable to their everyday lives in the contemporary world? How is it that people from many different cultural backgrounds read Homer's (c.) eighth-century-BC epic poem *Odyssey*, and Shakespeare's sixteenth- and seventeenth-century plays, relate to the characters, and see the behavior of these characters as reflecting on their own twenty-first-century lives? The answer is that we read and relate to great literature from centuries and even thousands of years ago, because of strong continuities and similarities in human psychological characteristics across time. Foundational similarities in human behavior persist over very long time periods, and this enables us to enjoy and benefit from great literature from past eras.[17] Of course, human societies change over time, particularly in terms of technology and science, but basic human behavior patterns persist.

Now, consider how we enjoy literature, and the arts more broadly, within time across cultures. How is it that works of twenty-first-century literature are translated and read by people belonging to many different cultures, even though the translated work of literature might be from a culture and a country that most readers will not have visited? To take an example from another field of art, how is it that there is now a huge international cinema market, so that films made in India, Nigeria, and many other countries are popular in societies outside where they were made? The answer is that the international cinema market relies on the same similarities in human characteristics that enable people to enjoy literature originating from other historical era and from other societies.

When we watch a movie made in Nigeria about people living in Nigerian society, of course we notice some differences in their behavior and culture, but we can understand what is being shown on the screen because of foundational human similarities. The relationships between family members and people from different generations, the emotions of young people romantically attracted to one another, the

---

[16] See readings in Eizadirad and Wane (2023).

[17] The concept of political plasticity reflects this kind of behavioral continuity in the political domain.

challenges faced by children growing up, and the sadness following the death of a loved one—there are similarities in these and many other experiences across many different societies. Although there will also be some variations and exceptions to each trend, the similarities are strong enough to enable us to understand the Nigerian movie we are watching. The vibrant international film market attests to this.

The experience of travel also provides support for the idea that there are foundational similarities across humanity. I am writing this chapter while I travel in India, which has overtaken China as the most populous country in the world. There are 22 scheduled (official) languages and numerous religions in this country of 1.4 billion people, 750 million of whom are 25 years and younger. The traveler moving across India encounters many different languages, religions, foods, clothing styles, and cultural practices. The geography and climate also vary considerably within India. To say that India is a diverse country is an understatement. However, despite all these variations, Indians successfully travel across their own country as tourists and also travel from region to region to engage in commerce, and travelers from outside India routinely communicate with and understand the people of India—even though they do not know local languages.

One of the genuine joys of international travel is the thrill of being in a country where one does not know the local people, language, and customs. Thrilling, but also frightening. How do strangers cope in such situations? The first thing we can say for certain is that travelers have successfully coped with such situations for thousands of years.[18] In the Western context, the adventures of Marco Polo (1254–1324) along the Silk Road are very well known. However, Ibn Battuta (1304–1369) is less well known in Wesern societies; this North African explorer is thought to have traveled for about 30 years over 79,000 miles across about 40 countries (on the twenty-first-century map).[19] There is a long history of people journeying to new lands, even when they do not speak the language(s) and know the customs of inhabitants in the new territories.

Also, think about our nomadic ancestors, prior to about 10,000 years ago, before we lived settled lives as farmers with domesticated animals. Human beings developed cumulative culture through extensive and continuous communications and information exchange between people.[20] Our nomadic ancestors exchanged information, for example, about the use of plants as food and as medicine, with others who did not necessarily speak the same language and share the same customs. Communication, information exchange, and trade were always ongoing between groups of strangers—and this was only possible because of the foundational similarities between human beings.

Just as in the past, in the twenty-first century similarities between human beings allow us to successfully interact with "outsiders." We can travel to foreign

---

[18] Gosch and Stearns (2007).

[19] Ibn Battutah (2003).

[20] Salali et al. (2016).

countries where we do not know the language and are unfamiliar with the local culture, but we nevertheless communicate, develop social relationships, and live among these strangers—sometimes for long time periods. This is only possible because of the very important similarities we have with all other humans. Their language, religion, clothing, food, and culture broadly could be different, but these differences are objectively far less foundational than the enormous similarities we have with them.

Concluding Comment

The enjoyment of world literature, cinema, and arts, as well as international travel, are among activities that testify to the similarities among humankind. Of course, we can choose to give priority to differences rather than similarities, even though we humans are far more similar to one another than we are different. We can choose to celebrate differences that are often exaggerated, and in some cases fabricated. This is the choice that has been made when societies adopt multiculturalism as a policy for managing diversity. But omniculturalism and the active celebration of human commonalities already has a solid foundation, and leads to more constructive outcomes. Our future survival requires a focus on our shared commonalities, rather than the manufacturing and celebration of differences.

References

Brinkmann, H., Commare, L., Leder, H., & Rosenberg, R. (2014). Abstract art as a universal language? *Leonardo, 47*, 256–257.
Campbell, J. (2003). *The hero's journey: Joseph Campbell on his life and work* (Vol. 7). New World Library.
Eizadirad, A., & Wane, N. N. (Eds.). (2023). *The power of oral culture in education*. Palgrave Macmillan.
Engler, S., & Whitesides, K. A. (2022). Emic concepts and etic paths. *Religion, 52*, 1–5.
Fukuyama, F. (1992). *The end of history and the last man*. Free Press.
Gosch, S. S., & Stearns, P. N. (2007). *Premodern travel in world history*. Routledge.
Haggar, N. (2012). *A new philosophy of literature: The fundamental theme and unity of world literature; The vision of the infinite and the universalist literary tradition*. O Books.
Hambly, G. (2021). The not so universal hero's journey. *Journal of Screenwriting, 12*, 135–150.
Harnad, S. (2017). To cognize is to categorize: Cognition is categorization. In H. Cohen & C. Lefebvre (Eds.), *Handbook of categorization in cognitive science* (pp. 21–54). Elsevier.
Ibn Battutah. (2003). *The travels of Ibn Battutah*. (Ed. T. Mackintosh-Smith). Picadore.
Johnson, M. (2016). *Human biology: Concepts and current issues* (8th ed.). Pearson.
Johnson, T. M., & Grim, B. J. (2013). *The world's religions in figures: An introduction to international religious demography*. John Wiley & Sons.
Kant, E. (2002). *Groundwork for the metaphysics of morals*. In A. W. Wood (Ed. & Trans.). Yale University Press. (Original work published 1785).

Kalat, J. W. (2022). *Introduction to psychology* (12th ed.). Cengage.

Marx, K., & Engels, F. (2021). *The communist manifesto*. Chump Change Edition. First published 1848.

McKee, R., & El-Wakil, B. (2022). *Action: The art of excitement for screen, page, and game*. Twelve.

Moghaddam, F. M. (2019). *Threat to democracy: The appeal of authoritarianism in an age of uncertainty*. American Psychological Association.

Salali, G. D., Chaudhary, N., Thompson, J., Grace, O. M., van der Burgt, X. M., Dyble, M., et al. (2016). Knowledge-sharing networks in hunter-gatherers and the evolution of cumulative culture. *Current Biology, 26*(18), 2516–2521.

Afterword: Omniculturalism, A "Must-Succeed" Project for All Humanity

Humankind has reached a historic turning point, one that is consequential for our very existence. Since the end of the Second World War, we have been dealing with the threat posed by nuclear proliferation: nine countries are estimated to have enough nuclear weapons to destroy the world as we know it.[1] We have struggled to manage the nuclear threat, but now we are confronted by an even more perilous danger, human-induced global warming.[2] Scientific research tells us that unless we change our behavior to alter the current course of global warming, we are under threat of extinction.[3] As Paul Ehrlich and Anne Ehrlich explain, "For decades, environmental scientists have warned of interconnected environmental trends, such as losses of plant and animal diversity, rapid climate change, and the spread of toxic chemicals over Earth, that, unless reversed, could ultimately bring down our civilization."[4] Affluent countries have the most responsibility, "…each baby born in the United States on average will cause 15–150 times more environmental damage than a baby born in a very poor country."[5]

How can we best organize ourselves to solve the problem of global warming? Certainly not by focusing on and celebrating differences between groups, and encouraging groups to keep on "discovering" new intergroup differences to celebrate. No, this is the wrong path. The problem of global warming can only be solved by making human commonalities the highest priority, and by teaching the young that human beings are far more similar to one another than they are different. Global warming confronts us all, and, to succeed, we must meet this challenge by focusing on our commonalities. Omniculturalism is the best path for all humanity; our survival depends on it.

---

[1] Kristensen et al. (2023).

[2] Abbass et al. (2022).

[3] Johansen (2023).

[4] Ehrlich and Ehrlich (2004, p. 7).

[5] Ehrlich and Ehrlich (2004, p. 115).

© The Editor(s) (if applicable) and The Author(s), under exclusive license to
Springer Nature Switzerland AG 2024
F. M. Moghaddam, *The Psychology of Multiculturalism, Assimilation, and Omniculturalism*, SpringerBriefs in Psychology,
https://doi.org/10.1007/978-3-031-62597-8

References

Abbass, K., Qasim, M. Z., Song, H., Murshed, M., Mahmood, H., & Younis, I. (2022). A review of the global climate change impacts, adaptation, and sustainable mitigation measures. *Environmental Science and Pollution Research, 29,* 42539–42559.

Ehrlich, P. R., & Ehrlich, A. H. (2004). *One with Nineveh: Politics, consumption and the human future.* Island Press.

Johansen, B. E. (2023). *Global warming and the climate crisis: Science, spirit, and solutions.* Springer.

Kristensen, H. M., Korda, M., Johns, E., & Knight, M. (2023). Nuclear weapons sharing, 2023. *Bulletin of the Atomic Scientists, 79*(6), 393–406.

Index

Printed in the USA
CPSIA information can be obtained
at www.ICGtesting.com
CBHW071908220724
11974CB00003B/89

9 783031 625961